The Natural Waterways
of Ireland

The Natural Waterways of Ireland

A Traveler's Guide to Rental Boating

by Michael and Laura Murphy

Interlink Books
An imprint of Interlink Publishing Group, Inc.
New York • Northampton

First published 2001 by
INTERLINK BOOKS
An imprint of Interlink Publishing Group, Inc.
99 Seventh Avenue • Brooklyn, New York 11215 and
46 Crosby Street • Northampton, Massachusetts 01060
www.interlinkbooks.com

Library of Congress Cataloging-in-Publication Data

Murphy, Michael, 1927–
    The natural waterways of Ireland : a traveler's guide to rental boating/
Michael and Laura Murphy
        p.   cm.
    ISBN 1-56656-381-X
    1. Boats and boating--Ireland--Guidebooks. 2. Waterways--Ireland--
Guidebooks. 3. Ireland--Guidebooks.
    I. Murphy, Laura.   II. Title.
GV776.467.I74 M87 2001
914.1504'824--dc21   00-013236

Printed and bound in Canada

To request our complete 44-page full-color catalog,
please call us toll free at **1-800-238-LINK,** visit our
website at **www.interlinkbooks.com**, or write to
Interlink Publishing
46 Crosby Street, Northampton, MA 01060
e-mail: info@interlinkbooks.com

Contents

Contents

Preface

Prior to 1996, we had never operated a boat larger than a skiff and outboard, so it was with mild apprehension that we loaded our luggage and groceries into our thirty-foot rented cabin cruiser, started the diesel engine and moved out of the boatyard at Carrick-on-Shannon into the waters of the great River Shannon. The following week was one of the most stimulating and gratifying of our lives.

We first learned about the existence of rental cabin cruisers and sailing yachts on European waters in 1989 while we were journeying through Great Britain working on a guidebook to vacation rentals. In the little town of Wroxham, Norfolk, just north of the cathedral city of Norwich and a little over a hundred miles northeast of London, the modern brick townhouse in which we were staying faced a strip of grass and a row of small trees that bordered a concrete quay. This, in turn, bordered a broad, slow-moving river. To our right a number of motor cruisers and sailboats were tied along several jetties that extended into the river. Although the boats were of various sizes and configurations, all flew the same flag insignia. We thought they belonged to members of a yacht club.

A young woman was cleaning a handsome motor cruiser that we judged to be some forty feet in length. To pass the time of day we inquired about the yacht club and the boats and were astonished to learn that they were not the pleasure craft of the well-to-do, they were for rent—for "hire" as the British say. They were hire cruisers available by the week (or short-breaks in the off-season) to anyone over eighteen years old who could pay the price and could see well enough to drive a car. Nothing was required: no license and no experience. Even the price was surprisingly modest—about that of a room in a decent London hotel. We were only familiar with canal narrowboats, so we didn't think they would actually turn over one of these $100,000 cruisers to us, we who had no motor-boating experience. But the reply was yes, indeed.

How would we learn about operating one, we asked, and find out about where to go. They would spend an hour or so with us, we were told, until we felt comfortable with what we were about to do. They would show us the switches and how to steer and tie up, go over the few rules, look at the charts and point out the many other boatyards along the routes, talk about safety, mention favorite pubs and inns and towns along the routes, help us select an itinerary if we wished, show us the pots, pans, dinnerware and bedding, cruise around a bit, demonstrate how to operate forward and reverse, tie the right knots at the moorings, and answer questions. She said no one traveled at high speed—these were tranquil journeys. They would suggest where to buy groceries in Wroxham. But not too many, she said—there are towns and shops along the way. And then they would hand us the keys.

We also learned that hire-boats are available not only the Broads and rivers of East Anglia, but on the great Shannon–Erne Waterway of Ireland, the clearwater Thames from London westward through the Heart of England, in Cambridgeshire, on the Avon, the Yorkshire Ouse, Lake Windermere and Loch Ness, and the long chain of lakes of the Scottish Highland.

The Broads beckoned, but we were on a land-bound four-month itinerary and could not sail off into the Norfolk sunrise. The vast waterlands remained in our thoughts, though, and we knew that the boats were waiting.

In 1995 we received a newsletter from the Northern Ireland Tourist Board excitedly announcing the re-opening of a mid-nineteenth-century canal connecting the fifty-mile long chain of lakes in County Fermanagh of Northern Ireland to the upper River Shannon in the Republic of Ireland, forming the largest natural waterway system of Europe, almost 300 miles between Belleek in the north and Limerick in the south, and including a number of large and scenically beautiful lakes.

Our previous interest in the project, the environmental care that had been taken, and the vastness of the river and lake system itself (not to mention the idea of taking the helm of a cabin cruiser) took us to Carrick-on-Shannon in 1996 on a magazine assignment. There we found tranquil waters flowing through Irish countryside that we had never seen before, forest-rimmed lakes remote from highways, waterbirds and wildlife in profusion, pretty waterside towns, inns, castle and abbey ruins, stately homes, and ancient monastic sites rarely visited by travelers by car or bus. In a word: Perfection.

Our Shannon–Erne adventure was soon followed by a return to England's Broads where it had all begun, to spend another splendid week, and to confirm that few Americans know about these vast *natural* lake and river systems of Europe, much less how to explore them. That, we felt, needed to be remedied, so we returned once more and began a water odyssey, a great near-circle that began at the south end of the Shannon, took us to the north of Scotland, and ended over two months later near the headwaters of the Thames.

We hope that this Shannon–Erne Waterway guide, as well our *The Natural Waterways of Great Britain*, will offer readers the means to see new sights, to see old sights from a new perspective and to know a different way of travel.

—Michael and Laura Murphy

IRELAND & THE
SHANNON-ERNE WATERWAY

Donegal

Belleek

Lower Lough Erne

Belfast

Enniskillen

Upper Lough Erne

Lough Allen

Lough Key

Shannon-Erne

Belturbet

Carrick-on-Shannon

Shannon

IRISH SEA

Lough Ree

River

Athlone

Galway

Dublin

Portumna

Banagher

THE ATLANTIC

Lough Derg

Shannon
Airport

Killaloe

Limerick

IRELAND

The Shannon - Erne Waterway

Cork

North

West ✦ East

South

EXAMPLE OF A NAVIGATION CHART

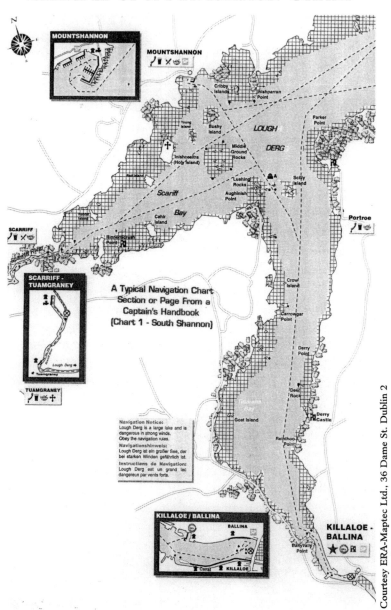

THE ERNE WATERWAY

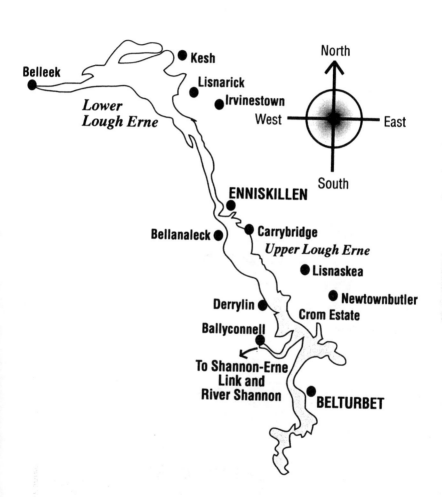

Kesh

Belleek

Lisnarick

Irvinestown

Lower Lough Erne

North

West ⊕ East

South

ENNISKILLEN

Bellanaleck

Carrybridge

Upper Lough Erne

Lisnaskea

Newtownbutler

Derrylin

Crom Estate

Ballyconnell

To Shannon-Erne Link and River Shannon

BELTURBET

The Natural Waterways of Ireland

THE SHANNON-ERNE LINK
(BALLINAMORE-BALLYCONNELL CANAL)

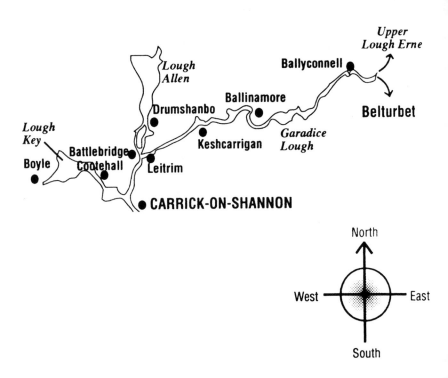

THE RIVER SHANNON WATERWAY

THE ERNE

THE SHANNON - ERNE LINK

Upper Lough Erne

Ballyconnell

Lough Allen

Drumshanbo

Ballinamore

Belturbet

Lough Key

Battlebridge
Cootehall

Keshcarrigan

Garadice Lough

Boyle

Leitrim

Shannon-Erne Link

CARRICK-ON-SHANNON
Drumsna

Jamestown

Dromod

N O R T H   S H A N N O N

ROOSKY

North

Tarmonbarry

Clondra

West ——— East

LANESBOROUGH

South

Inny River

Lecarrow

Lough Ree

Hodson Bay

Glasson

Ballykeeran

ATHLONE

Clonmacnois

S O U T H   S H A N N O N

Shannonbridge

Grand Canal

Shannon Harbour

BANAGHER

PORTUMNA

Lough Derg

Terryglass

Williamstown

Kilgarvan

Mountshannon

Dromineer

Scarriff

Garrykennedy

KILLALOE

CHAPTER 1

Introduction

The term *Shannon–Erne Waterway* is the name given to the entire system of connected rivers and lakes and the short canal that forms a continuous navigable stretch of waters nearly 300 miles (485 km) in length, making it the longest natural waterway in Europe open to navigation by small craft. Indeed, small craft navigation is its primary use. From the town of Belleek near Donegal Bay on the northwest coast of Northern Ireland to the Shannon estuary west of Limerick in the southwest of the Republic of Ireland, the waterway flows in the shape of a question-mark across virtually the entire country. It flows in two directions from the divide in the low mountains that lie roughly along the political border between Northern Ireland and the Republic, through countrysides of varied topography and past the evidences of history dating from the stone age up to the towns of modern Ireland.

The four sections of the waterway—The Erne Lakes & River System, the Shannon–Erne Link, the North Shannon, and the South Shannon—are presented in the chapters from north to south, but this does not suggest that this needs to be your direction of travel. Indeed, within each of the regional sections the sequence of stops on suggested itineraries may be in any direction and actually tend to more "upstream" than down. Since the direction of cruising is immaterial, the key is to choose a section of the waterway that interests you,

1

and that you can handle in the time you have available. For vacationers who have one or two weeks at best, the descriptions of the four regions will suggest itineraries from which one or two regions can be chosen or prioritized. Following a brief overview of the waterway's four distinct segments:

• *The River Erne and Erne Lakes*: The Erne flows northwesterly from the hills of County Cavan in the Republic, opening into the slender, island-filled Upper Lough Erne, narrowing, then opening again at Enniskillen into the broad Lower Lough Erne. The main towns on this part of the waterway are Belturbet at the upper end of Erne River navigation, Enniskillen near the middle, and Belleek near the Atlantic at the downstream end. Crom Castle lies at the juncture of the Erne and Woodford River at the northern end of the Canal link. The Erne region is characterized by forests and islands, excellent coarse fishing, wildlife sanctuaries, and monastic ruins.

• *The Shannon–Erne Link*: A wandering canal comprised of lakes, open river, canalized parts of the river, and manmade cuts. It includes the towns of Leitrim, Ballinamore, Ballyconnell; forests, many moorings, concentrations of swans, and sixteen electric/hydraulic locks.

• *The North Shannon*: The upper Shannon is the lower end of the Shannon–Erne Link, in the Republic's County Leitrim. Lough Allen and Lough Key are accessible by cruiser off the north Shannon, north of the main town, Carrick-on-Shannon. At the downriver (southern) end of this section is the town of Athlone. The North Shannon features hilly countryside that becomes more flat downriver, the large Lough Ree and the Inner Loughs, abundant birdlife, and excellent fishing. There are four locks along the entire section, including one on the River Boyle that runs into the North Shannon from Lough Key, all have lockkeepers.

• *The South Shannon:* Here, you will find large Lough Derg with pretty bays and inlets, high concentrations of birdlife, trophy pike, rolling forested hills becoming flatter toward the north, and one of the great monastic sites in Europe at Clonmacnois (Cluain Mhic Nóis). The main towns are, from north to south, Banagher, Portumna, Mt. Shannon, and Killaloe near Limerick. There is only one lock on this section, with lockkeeper. Killaloe is at present the south end of Shannon navigation, but plans are being laid to extend south to Limerick.

A Short History of the Shannon–Erne Waterway

The history of the Shannon and of the Erne must start in antiquity, with even the more "modern" manifestations—the remains of monastic communities, high crosses, ancient abbeys, and round towers—dating from the seventh and eighth centuries. These historic places, along with wildlife, villages, and towns, are among the riches to be discovered on a cruise along the Shannon, the Erne, and the Ballinamore–Ballyconnell Canal, now appropriately called the Shannon–Erne Link.

There are many towns and villages along the waterway whose origins lie in the distant past, as well as a few that in the past decade or two have grown into bustling modern communities, yet still retain the traces of their past, seen in stately houses, castles, ancient-but-still-used churches, old inns, and pubs. Information on many of these is contained in the respective regional chapters, and much more is available in the boatyard and tourist offices after arrival in Ireland.

The Shannon–Erne Link, or Ballinamore–Ballyconnell Canal as it was formerly called, is a remarkable tale of fairly contemporary history. For over a century it lay in hopeless ruin, choked with vegetation, the stone walls of the locks' chambers collapsed, wooden lock gates rotted. Built between 1847 and 1858, the canal was a colossal project involving thousands of workmen with only rudimentary tools. Created both for drainage and to open a north-south waterway linking other completed inland navigations, the canal was to be an artery for moving everything from Guinness stout to roofing tile, including the coal used to fire the kilns at Belleek, and then the famed Belleek china that came out of those kilns on to the markets of England and the Continent. But instead, the canal became a nightmare. Within a few years of completion the canal died, done in by technical problems and the new railway. No wonder then that in the late 1980s the decision was not lightly made to reconstruct the great meandering canal. Ultimately, £30,000,000 (US$46 million) was jointly committed by the governments of the United Kingdom, the Republic of Ireland, and the European Regional Fund. The result is not only an attractive, environmentally sound, tranquil connection through the mountains of north-central Ireland, but the creation of the longest and most beautiful natural non-commercial waterway of Europe.

The Geography

From the apex of the watershed at Lough Scur in the mountains of counties Leitrim and Fermanagh, the stream direction of the Woodford River is northeasterly to where it joins the River Erne, which in turn flows north-northwest into Northern Ireland and across County Fermanagh. The Ballinamore–Ballyconnell Canal, now simply called the Link, flows almost east-west.

On the southern side of the watershed, the legendary River Shannon flows southward 212 miles (345 km) from its headwaters through the physical heart of Ireland, forming a wide estuary near the southern city of Limerick. The 170-mile (275-km) navigable portion of the Shannon and its lake system comprises some 770 square miles (2,035 sq km). For purposes of navigation as well as description, the guide will refer to the two watersheds or drainages as the north (Erne) and the south (Shannon).

Introduction

When first planning the design of this guidebook there were to be three chapters devoted to the Shannon–Erne: one on the Republic of Ireland's River Shannon, one on Northern Ireland's River Erne and Erne Lakes, and one on the Shannon–Erne Link, the canal and river system that connects the two through the low mountains that run along the border. But our journeys made clear that there is geographic continuity of the whole waterway; the connecting Shannon–Erne Link is a successful cross-border enterprise. The waterways and tourist organization authorities look upon the Shannon–Erne as a unified whole.

Regardless of political boundaries, the waterway is indeed one, treated in the guidebook as separate chapters only in order to help visitors with limited time to cruise (less than three weeks) to choose where to spend their time. As for the border, the remains of a blown bridge stand on each side of the Woodford north of Ballinamore, but they have stood there for many years, and there is now no other sign of a border.

The approximate one-way non-stop cruising time between Killaloe at the south end of the waterway and Belleek at the north is 51 hours, though a bit slower northbound and a bit faster southbound due to stream flows. That's a little over three days of relentless cruising during summer daylight and five days in winter when the days are shorter. Nor does 51 hours allow for sleeping, or side trips into Lough Key, or Lough Allen, up the Erne to Belturbet, or exploring the inner lakes of Lough Ree, stops at Clonmacnois, or at the dolmen and Finn McCools's burial site at Keshkerrigan, or the monastic ruins on Devenish, White, and Inishmacsaint islands. Realistically, then, two-and-a-half to three weeks of cruising and exploration at a leisurely pace should be planned for the entire waterway. But taking a one- or two-week segment may be the best approach, and any of several options are possible. But which? That depends on individual interests and to some extent on individual capacities.

5

Best Times to Go

Ireland's waterway is less subject to crowding than most of the natural waterways of England, and is in fact more dependent on the vacation schedules of Continental Europeans, especially Germans, than other factors except opening days of fishing season and various fishing derbies and competitions. In general, however, considering climate as well as European tourist travel, May, early June, and September are optimum. April and October can be beautiful times, but the chance of rain and inclement weather is greater, especially in the north. Although the south is slightly warmer, the entire island is not so large that climactic differences should influence plans for early and late season travel.

Advance Booking Time

The greater the advance time, the better the selection of boats. The first to go are the larger cruisers that sleep six or more; these are taken mainly by parties of anglers from the Continent. Play it safe and for July and August book three months in advance; for May, early-June, and September, two months; for other times, two to three weeks. If you happen to pick a time when some major fishing event has absorbed the best boats, ask the boatyard for the best dates near to your selected time—it will usually be an adjustment of only a few days or a week.

Free-Cruising vs. Canals & Narrowboats

Free-Cruising is the term we use to describe travel by motor cruiser on open waterways. In fact, for purposes of this guidebook, the reference is to open *natural* waterways, which in Ireland is the 300-mile length of the Shannon–Erne Waterway, except for a 37-mile (60-km) long section called the Shannon–Erne Link. The Link is part hand-constructed canal and partly the Woodford River, making this relatively

6

short section part natural and part handmade. There is a small narrowboat operation based in the Link, but the Link is principally used by motor cruisers moving between the Shannon headwaters at the south end and the River Erne at the north.

Narrowboats are aptly named, constructed to fit within the confines of canals, such as the Grand Canal that connects the Dublin area with the Shannon, and that crisscross Britain. Although there are canal/narrowboat operations in Ireland, this guide deals with cabin cruisers and natural waters.

For natural-water cruising, many motor cruiser designs are of broader beam, and they offer a variety of configurations, including the familiar design we see in marinas around the US and Canada. They are comfortable vessels that are free to move wherever you wish: you plan the itinerary and control the helm. Itineraries, directions, and mooring spots are open to choice, especially on the vast lakes formed by the Shannon in the Republic of Ireland, and the Erne lakes of Northern Ireland. Even on the Shannon–Erne Link, the traffic is light and much of the canal is actually the wandering Woodford River. In a nutshell, free-cruising differs from canal boating by providing freedom to go where you want and when you want and to go at your own pace (so long as it's slow) and to moor where you please. It's a matter of independence. All the vessels are built for ease of handling, maneuverability, and comfort rather than speed, and provide the ultimate way for exploring the waters and the countryside, combining a place to live with a means of travel.

The Purpose of this Guide

When considering any new adventure, the difficulty for most travelers, beginners and experienced alike, is how to decide exactly where to spend their journey. The three regions of the Ireland's natural waterway noted earlier in this chapter combine to make a system so lengthy and expansive that they cannot all be thoroughly explored in the span of an average vacation. But a week or two for the first adventure is ample, leaving some waters and explorations for another time.

One purpose, then, is to help in making the choice by describing the features of each of the areas: Their geographic and topographic nature, an overview of their wildlife and flora, their historical character in terms of monastic sites, towns and villages, abbeys, castles and the like, as well as the waters themselves. The variety of itineraries and the best times to go will help in planning and, finally, we provide a short overview of the hospitality of the region to boaters in terms of waterside pubs, grocers, fuel, and other support, and general access to places of interest.

We also introduce the companies and the boats. For seasoned sailor and beginner alike, there are the details about how to obtain information, how to choose among the many types and sizes of cruisers and what is included under the rental agreements, costs, the terms of insurance, and damage deposits. Each chapter will provide an overview of the boats available in the region, what charts are important and how to obtain them, and how to book and pay for the rental. The guide will explain how the short on-site introduction to boating and training takes place. Support services on the waterway are noted, along with particular boatyards and boats that seem best for travelers from abroad.

To many Irish, Britons, and Continentals, renting a boat for a week on the waters of Ireland, Great Britain, and France is only slightly more unusual than renting a car. For most North Americans, however, not only is the whole idea of such water exploration by rental cruisers new, but the process of making wise choices and arranging the booking from this side of the Atlantic may seem daunting. It is not, and this guide is designed to make it both understandable and achievable.

How to Use this Guide

Unless you know precisely where you want to go—which part or parts of this long waterway—an hour or so perusing the guidebook will be a good beginning. If you have a specific destination in mind, say on the Erne lakes of County Fermanagh, simply go directly to the appropriate chapter. In general, however, choices must be made: river or lake, wildlife sanctuaries, fishing areas, regions where the social life of waterside pubs, inns and towns call, or where monastic ruins rising from islands tell of other times? All of these, or some of these?

A look at the highlights of the regions summarized in this introductory chapter will provide a sense of the general nature of four regions of the waterway and the countryside in which they lie. These are expanded upon in each of the regional chapters, adding detail and calling attention to the more important points along the route: the wildlife areas, towns, inns, castles, and ruins that should not be missed. Because the Shannon–Erne regions differ from one another in terms of area or length or magnitude or shape, it follows that there may not be consistency in the order of subjects as they unfold in each chapter. In general, however, each chapter begins with an overview that describes in general terms the topography of the area, the nature of the waterways, their scope and expanse, and recommendations on how long should be allotted for a reasonable itinerary. Although this is not a naturalist's handbook, each chapter includes a short overview of the regions's flora and wildlife, including information on the flyways and specific areas within the region where, for example, birders will likely be rewarded, or unusual plants may be found. And in addition to the natural character of the waterway regions, the overview also touches upon the human history of these areas.

If the overview of the topography, history, and nature of the waters and the countryside piques your curiosity, then go on to read about the highlights of the region. For if the overview, for example, tells that Ireland's lower River Shannon flows gently and wide through rolling countryside, forming Loch Derg, the highlights will then tell of a sanctuary on Lough Derg where a remarkable variety of bird species attracts bird watchers from throughout Europe. The highlights are narrative descriptions of specific sections of rivers, lakes or mixed waterways in terms of special things to watch for: outstanding bird area, inviting woods to walk through, castle or abbey to explore, outstanding pub or inn for lunch or dinner, or pleasant overnight mooring. This information can often be enhanced by use of general guidebooks to the country or region, books that deal more specifically with such topics as natural history and environmental studies.

The chapters tell about the water journey in general, written in a manner to provide a sense of what it will be like. These are the subjective views of the authors as American visitors, exploring not only the countryside, but also the actuality of boating abroad. Once a segment of the system is decided upon, the detailed waterway navigational chart and guide may be purchased from the suitable Irish source shown in the applicable chapter, as noted. These charts indicate every spot to tie up, every town along the route, locks if any, and most ancient sites to visit.

Self-discovery and exploration of a watercourse is part of the fun, and poring over these navigation charts or talking with boatyard staff is the best approach to the journey. And finding out where to go becomes easier as each day passes, even on the larger and more complex waterways. Nevertheless, there are situations and places where an example of how time might be allotted, distances covered, stops at important sites figured in, and even nighttime moorings to aim for, is helpful, especially at the beginning. Where the waterway system, or the region, is such that an illustration or two will help in planning, then a sample itinerary or two is provided. Again, these offer ideas, and are not meant to be followed at the expense of exploring some unmentioned backwater, village, or ruin.

The section in each chapter on the cruiser lines describes a selection of recommended companies that are most easily reached by foreign travelers without rental cars. Other criteria include the quality of the boatyards, the cruisers themselves, and the service. Other considerations are the ease by which groceries and supplies can be purchased nearby, and the location of the marina relative to the most desirable cruising areas.

In addition to general information later in this introduction, information about getting to the boatyards is generally provided in the section about the boat companies and will explain the best approach to finding the boatyards, especially for travelers who do not have a car. Often, it is simply a matter of telling the company where and when you are arriving in Ireland, and they will arrange transportation. Shannon or Dublin are the assumed destination airports in the Republic of Ireland, and for Northern Ireland either Belfast or Dublin. If you rent a car, ask the boat rental company or agent to provide a road map and directions along with the booking documents that will be sent to you.

In the section on the cruiser companies, we will also discuss reasons to prefer one rental company over another. For example, if a one-way itinerary is planned, you will want a company that has boatyard bases at the desired starting and ending points. We will also note where we were especially impressed with a particular fleet of cruisers, or some classic styles, for those who favor traditional craft. If there are any reasons why one style of cruiser might be preferable to another, these also will be discussed in this section. For example, some boat designs are better suited to children, from a perspective of safety or convenience. Some designs are more comfortable in seasons of marginal weather, some especially suited to hot weather cruising, some especially suited to disabled persons. Please note that when discussing size of the boats, we use the notation 4+2, for example, to mean that the boat has four berths (may be double and twin, two doubles or two twins) plus a convertible arrangement that sleeps two.

To Novices, Newcomers, & All

Who can take the helm? In two words: almost anyone. Experience not required! A person must be over eighteen years of age and in reasonably good health (sixteen when accompanied by an adult). For persons with no boating experience, the staff of the rental company will provide a hands-on training session at the time of boat pickup. There is nothing about the operation and navigation of the rental motor cruisers that cannot be learned from scratch in about two hours. Enough time will be spent training to assure that the boat can be handled properly and safely. It is, after all, in the owners' interest to make sure that their $30,000 to $200,000 investments don't wind up in somebody's yard or athwart a pier piling.

The charts provided by the boat renters are very detailed, and interpreting them is self-evident. Markers on the charts are accurately keyed to the navigation symbols posted in the various waterways, so it's easy to always know precisely where you are. Only once did we go astray, misreading our chart and turning too soon into what we thought was a broad channel between islands in Ireland's Upper Loch Erne. It was instead a shallow bay and we were soon stuck fast on the lake bottom. We lightened the boat in stages, first by putting our heaviest luggage in the dinghy, followed by groceries and finally one of us. It worked—we eased our way out. Despite our success, as we cleared the bay we saw a boat heading toward us, obviously coming to help. When they saw that we were free they came about, waved, and returned toward the marina.

There is always someone to lend a hand. Rangers keep an eye and discreetly patrol the entire length of the

Introduction

Shannon–Erne Link. When we left the upper Shannon and entered the canal that connects it with the Erne Lakes, we were met at the first lock by a blue-uniformed ranger who seemed to appear from nowhere. He said he knew we were coming, then went through the entire operation with us, showing us everything from how to insert our card into the automatic lock console, to how to toss and secure the lines. He said there was a ranger on each end of the Link to coach new boaters in the procedure.

Except for stormy days on the two large lakes of the Shannon and Lower Lough Erne, the Waterway is calm, the current manageable; the atmosphere that prevails among boaters is that of relaxation. People are going places at a slow speed; there is much stopping, bird-watching, photographing, identifying shore plants, tying up to walk a waterside path or explore a ruin. Pauses at waterside pubs or inns, at docks in quaint market villages, at parks, at castles, and the ruins of monastic communities pleasantly absorb all the time that isn't spent cruising, eating, and sleeping. There are no races or high-speed runs; roaring engines are not allowed. Boating of this kind in the UK and in Ireland is seen as a civilized pursuit, a means of experiencing places otherwise inaccessible, traveling quietly through natural habitat. With a week to travel perhaps 120 miles (195 km), there is no rush. Even beginners will feel quite relaxed, as well as delighted, by the end of the first day out.

The Training: A Summary of Instruction

Even experienced operators will be introduced to the boating area, charts and chart reading, safety procedures, and the mechanics of the cruiser, and will be taken out for a short operational overview. For novices, the training will be somewhat longer and instructions of a more basic nature will be included, such as:

Assignment of tasks for the crew. Even if there are only two persons, both must be able to take the helm and both must understand the deck and dock work necessary to moor, cast off, and handle any locks that may be encountered.

Starting the cruiser and the operation of the throttle and gearbox (most cruisers have only a one-handle combined throttle and gearbox for forward and reverse).

Reading the simple gauges and what they mean and what to do should they indicate a problem.

Knots: how to tie the proper hitch (there are really only two to memorize) so that the boat can be securely tied to the bollard, cleat, or ring, or any waterside post or tree, for that matter.

Lines: Handling of the mooring lines, emphasizing that they must pass UNDER any on-boat rails when mooring.

Mooring: You'll learn steering, speed, and direction control for mooring, and will understand the importance of approaching moorings with the boat headed upstream. This gives maximum steering control and enables you to bring the boat to a very slow speed, or even a dead stop, when the upriver speed of the boat equals the speed of the current. Our first instructor observed that when your boat isn't moving it's hard to incur any damage. If you approach the dock, wharf, or pier at less than a mile per hour, it's easy for the person with the deck assignment to step ashore and tie up. If you are headed downstream, simply pass by the mooring point, make a U-turn and approach with the bow pointed upstream.

Introduction

In addition to the video and the hands-on instruction, each "Captain's Handbook" contains point-by-point details on everything from checking-in to CPR and what to do if you run aground. Again, you are never alone. There are always other boaters to lend a hand, always a ranger or a boatyard staff member keeping an eye out. If the weather should turn foul, either moor or, if not possible, keep other boats in sight.

The Work Involved

Although there is not much physical effort required, there are nonetheless activities that demand attention and a modicum of work. Locks are the cause for most of the labor, and although there are far fewer than encountered by narrowboats on the canals, there are occasional ones on the Shannon, and a number on the Link.

The few Shannon locks are large, easy-to-manage, and all are operated by a lockkeeper. They provide, in fact, a nice break, a chance to talk with other boaters, to walk about, to chat with the affable keepers.

All the locks on the newly rebuilt Link are automatic, triggered by a plastic card like a phone card or door opener, demonstrating the use of technology in modern lock operations. The main effort is stepping ashore, walking up a grassy slope, and then pushing buttons on a stainless steel console that stands beside the lock wall. It is not difficult and will be described later in the book (Chapter 3, The Shannon–Erne Link). The procedure will also be explained by boatyard staff before your departure, and again at the first lock.

We do not want to minimize the fact that in some areas a little effort is needed, but the leisurely pace doesn't call for heroic effort. For example, our first voyage up the Shannon–Erne Link and its sixteen automatic locks was one of the most interesting parts of the journey. True, on the night we moored at the by-way at Keshcarrigan Lock we felt quite ready to retire, but it was a good, healthy tiredness. We settled in and listened to the boat's radio play a tribute to Ella Fitzgerald.

Cruiser Rental Companies & Agents

The basic consideration in the choice of company is which stretch or stretches of the waterway you plan to cruise. The boat companies are individually profiled in the appropriate sections following, but because this is such a lengthy waterway, it serves a useful purpose to initially deal with the fleets and their locations more generally.

Seventeen boat companies operate marinas with rental cruisers along the overall waterway, most of them profiled in the regional chapters. Of these, four operate from two or more boatyards, thus offering the option of one-way cruises, a distinct advantage to foreign visitors who do not arrive with a car that must be left at one point and picked up after the cruise. These companies and their boatyard locations make possible an extended linear itinerary rather than a round-trip cruise:

Carrick Craft: Banagher (S. Shannon), Carrick-on-
Shannon (N. Shannon), Knockninny (Erne)
Emerald Star-Connoisseur: Portumna (S. Shannon),
Carrick-on-Shannon (N. Shannon), Belturbet (Erne)
Erincurrach Cruising: Blaney (Lower Lough Erne),
paired with Shannon Erne Waterway Holidays Ltd.,
Knockvicar, River Boyle (N. Shannon)

It is not uncommon to see cruisers of these companies most anywhere along the route, meaning that boaters are likely to be on one-way trips, but neither is it rare to see boats from distant single-operation boatyards, meaning that the boaters are at the extreme end of a three- or four-week round trip itinerary. We visited with boaters as far south as Portumna who had departed from an Erne boatyard two weeks before, and would require two weeks to return. We also spotted occasional cruisers in the Erne lakes whose bases were far to the south. This extended round-trip approach tends, however, to be uncommon, so it may be that there are boaters who prefer to cruise eight hours or longer each day virtually non-stop. Our inclination is not toward marathon cruising, and our recommendation is to take it easy. There is much to enjoy along the way.

For those traveling without a car, the one-way approach has the advantage of providing exploration of the maximum linear distance possible. On the other hand, much can be said in favor of concentrating on one area or section of the waterway, exploring in depth, spending more time in waterside villages, historic sites, fishing, or even stopping for an afternoon of golf. Further, on a return trip there is much new to be seen, and places can be re-visited that seemed appealing outbound, making them familiar and easy to manage on the return.

Once travelers decide which section of the Shannon–Erne to explore, the time comes to choose the boat company and the vessel. We feel that for many visitors *convenience* is most important. It doesn't make sense, for example, to travel 120 miles (195 km) from Dublin airport to some remote boatyard where there is no grocery store or other facilities, especially when there are fleets that are better located and other boat companies to choose from. With this in mind, we have paid special attention to those boat companies that best fit four criteria:

1. Convenient to destination airports.
2. Located in or near population centers where there are lodgings, pubs, and restaurants and, most important, a grocery store within easy walking distance of the marina (or one that will deliver or fill orders placed with the boat company).

3. Located in spots from which the most interesting itineraries can be carried out.

4. Having a good selection of cruisers, a well-maintained fleet, fair prices, and the ability to provide full support and service to their clients.

The boat companies that best meet these criteria are profiled in detail later in the regional chapters, with each profile including how best to start your voyage, accommodations in the vicinity, ideal itineraries and the best nearby moorings.

The decision to book directly with the rental boat company, with one of the British brokerage companies (Blakes or Hoseasons), or with a US agent, depends in part on how much time and effort you want to put into your planning, and whether or not you want to talk with someone in the US who can make recommendations that will best suit your needs. The easiest way to gather information on specific boats and their cost is to peruse their internet websites or, better, to obtain copies of the enticing and wonderfully descriptive color catalogs. They cover every waterway and describe and picture a vast array of types, sizes, and quality standards of boat. It also means that rather than dealing with dozens of boatyards there are a few single sources for obtaining information and, finally, one company to book through and to pay (credit cards accepted). This makes the process very easy, especially when doing the planning from overseas. Each regional chapter contains information on how to obtain the catalog.

Contacting the boat company directly has the advantage of being able to communicate with someone on the scene: a person who intimately knows the cruisers, the boatyard, the surroundings, and the waterway. Most of the companies have brochures with cruiser photographs and layouts as well as the price list, and many have their own website. A phone conversation with boatyard proprietors or staff will likely be helpful whether you book directly with them or through a US or British agent. We feel this is especially true with cruiser companies on the Shannon–Erne Waterway.

The US-based agents we include in the Appendix should have had experience traveling the various regions and should offer ideas and suggestions, as well as make catalogs and brochures available more quickly than waiting for delivery from overseas. These agents must, of course, cover their costs of domestic advertising, telephone, processing of the financial dealings with the boat companies and the like, so expect to pay a slight commission for these services rendered. How much? Ask them. For many travelers, especially first-time boaters, a small fee may be worth it even if it's just for the peace of mind from dealing "locally."

As for dealing with regular travel agents, very few have seen, much less operated, these motor cruisers, yet there is almost always an additional commission involved. In fact, there may be two commission steps because the travel agent often goes through a US or Canadian boat agent, who in turn represents the European companies.

Choosing the Right Motor Cruisers

The variety of motor cruisers available for rent is astonishing. Among the motor vessels in Ireland the basic configurations are: (1) the aft-cockpit cruiser, (2) the center-cockpit cruiser, (3) the forward-drive cruiser, and (4) the flybridge-style cruiser with dual helms. These come in all configurations and sizes, some with sliding roof, some with sliding canopy, some with glass doors to the sundeck, some with one full bathroom (with shower), others with two, some with separate shower, others with two toilet rooms and a separate shower and so forth. The smallest sleep two and are about 26 feet in length, with a 9-foot beam. The largest sleep ten in five separate cabins, have two showers and three toilets and boast a 48-foot length and a 12-plus-foot beam. There is practically every size, combination and configuration in between. All have complete and fully-equipped galleys as well as all kitchenware and dinnerware needed to match the needs of the number of people on board. Most include color TV, but some cost a small extra fee.

In the catalogs, and many websites, the boat photographs and written descriptions are accompanied by a diagram of the boat layout. They show the relative size and the placement of all the rooms (cabins), galley, salon, cockpit, head (WC), cubbies, and usually even the placement of the cabinets, refrigerator, tables, and berths.

Although it depends somewhat on configuration, as a basic rule we recommend renting a boat rated to sleep more persons than will actually be cruising together. The price difference to step up one notch is relatively small and, we feel, is well worth it. Crowding diminishes the enjoyment. Also, consider a larger boat if you are planning for more than one week. A couple cruising for a week, for example, should rent a boat that sleeps three to four, ideally at least a 29-by-10-foot craft. A couple with a child will also do well in this size cruiser if there is not too much luggage.

With a few exceptions (Lochside on Lough Erne, for example), most boat companies stretch the number of persons their boats can accommodate. This isn't intentional, but not being used to boaters from across the Atlantic they rarely think about space for extra luggage and clothing. They are also used to travelers from the Continent, some of whom have cars, and many of whom don't seem to be as accustomed to spare space as are Americans and Canadians. Whatever the reason, don't simply take the figures for the number of berths as the defining factor for your boat selection. Look at layout, look at beam as well as length, and consider well the composition of your family or group. Study the configurations in the brochures or the website, mentally place each crew member in a berth, look for space for luggage (spare berth or spare cabin), and determine the crew's need for toilets and showers. Look at the photos as well as the diagrams for outside deck space in which to have morning coffee, lunch, fish, or just soak up the sun. Look, too, for a covering or canopy extending over the aft deck where it's possible to stand protected from rain; also imagine cruising in the rain when you consider the inner space.

Now, the price list. Find the price band or price code for the maximum of your budget for the time of year you want to rent (it may be a number like 25 or 67). Again, remember that other than the first and possibly last nights no hotel or other accommodation will be required, and that a rental car is not needed. Finally, peruse the catalog or website, marking the vessels which look good to you, which accommodate the number in your group or family, and which show a price band number equal to or less than the number you have budgeted for. From these boats, pick and rank several with the configuration and general appearance that most appeal to you, and let the company know by phone, fax, or e-mail of your decision. They will then let you know which boats are available at the specified time.

We tried Ireland Line's Birchwood 320 out of Killaloe, a 32-by-11 foot cruiser, and found it quite adequate, but for two couples it would have been a tight fit, despite being rated for four persons (and having four berths). For about $210 more ($30/day) one could take the spacious Birchwood 33, which would be luxury for four but a bit tight for six. The two of us luxuriated in Carrick Craft's Kilkenny class, a modern yet warmly finished wide-beam 34-foot cruiser set up for four to six persons. We wanted to try our hand at a heavier craft and so took it up some narrow sections north of Banagher on the south Shannon, through the Athlone lock and the fast water above the Athlone weir, and even weathered the tail end of Hurricane Andrew as we crossed Lough Ree. It was maneuverable, well laid out and overall a pleasure, excellent for four, a bit tight for six, lovely for two.

A caveat: With few exceptions, cruisers on the Shannon–Erne are of traditional design, with either aft cockpit or dual steering positions. There are, however, a few older narrowboat-like cruisers with sliding roof and forward drive like most found on England's Norfolk Broads. These are fine for open waters, but for the rivers these, they should, in our view, be avoided—especially by inexperienced boaters. Their advantage of providing a large volume of space for their dimensions is overshadowed by their limited view from the helm, especially toward the stern, plus long narrow external walkways alongside the cabin, making it hard to move quickly from the stern to the bows. This can be awkward, especially if you are only a two-person crew, or if there are children. Stick to the conventional designs, familiar in North American marinas. If you want the larger interior space, tell the agent or boatyard that you want to assure good rear viewing (as on the more modern sliding top cruisers).

We especially like cruisers with two helm positions and, in addition to the smaller aft cockpit cruisers, recommend them for novices. For very large cruisers, look for those with bow-thrusters (or ask the boatyard operator).

Comments on special regional designs as well recommen-dations for selections best suited for the various waterways will be found in the appropriate chapters on the individual waterways.

Rental Prices & Overall Costs

The specifics are contained in each of the appropriate area chapters, but rental prices range in the neighborhood of the cost of a vacation apartment in London or Dublin, and well below that of city hotel rooms of equal standards. Just as prices for hotel rooms, apartments, and other accommodations, boat prices are dependent on two factors: size and quality standards. The size factor is self-explanatory, and the standard has to do with the quality of the boat fittings, decor,

Introduction

furnishings, spaciousness, and, sometimes, age of the vessel. One company assigns ratings: standard, 3-star, 4-star and Blue Chip. It is also easy to scan the catalogs and websites to compare the size, layout, and appearance of the various boats with the price band or price group number always shown with the description. The fact is that you get what you pay for. With so many boatyards, competition is tough. If two boats are of the same size, same type and similar appearance, yet one rents for $500 per week and the other for $700 per week in the same season, the latter will usually be the most comfortable, convenient, and of a higher standard whether it is rated superior or not.

The range of prices, like the standards, is considerable, from economy to high. Nevertheless, we have been consistently impressed by the comparatively modest prices and excellent value for these vessels—hotel rooms are invariably much more. Our very modest hotel room in Carrick-on-Shannon, for example, cost about US$110 per night, the equivalent of some $100 per week higher than our 28-foot cruiser. Across the Irish Sea, the price of a room for two at London's Hyatt Carlton Tower, the Grosvenor, the Savoy, and the Sheraton Park Tower averages £1,650 (about US$2,350) per week. The most expensive motor cruiser on the Shannon, a 48-foot luxury vessel that accommodates ten persons in five separate cabins, rents for about IRE£1,250 (about US$1,375) per week in the peak months of July and August and the equivalent of $1,200 in June and September (and lower yet in the off-season). That's under $50 per day per couple.

Fuel is extra, but we were surprised to learn that a combination of engine efficiency, hull design, and the relatively slow pace of cruising on most of these waters keep the cost quite low. Diesel costs will run between IRE£6 and £10 per day (US$45 to $75 per week), depending on the size of the vessel and the speed at which it is operated.

Remember that the boat is both the vehicle and the

accommodation, as well as the place for breakfast and any other meals "in." Required cancellation and holiday insurance will run about $50, but insurance on the boat is included in the price. If you drive to the boatyard and leave the car, the cost will range from zero to $20 for parking (more information on getting to the boatyards in each of the regional chapters).

In sum, a family of four with modest requirements, or two couples sharing, can enjoy a week in a spacious motor cruiser with two sleeping cabins for under US$1,100 during the two peak months, $800 in June and September and $700 in other months, everything included except food and beverage. Add roughly $100 per week for the same size vessel but of luxury standard. A final cost to figure in is the price for at least a few meals ashore. For most travelers, the inviting nature of many of the waterside pubs and inns is too compelling to resist.

Mooring fees vary, but most of them are free at any of the many boatyards and marinas associated with each particular boat rental company. Fees at public moorings are also either free or cost very little. Basically, boaters are welcome and mooring and support are free.

On the 37-mile (60-km) long Shannon–Erne Link, boaters purchase an electronic card at the boatyard office for about IRE£20 (about US$25) that provides twenty "units." It takes one unit to operate each automatic lock, two units to operate the laundry facilities at moorings along the way, and one unit for full bathroom and shower facilities at the moorings in case larger showers than those on board are occasionally desired. (Warning: the sixteen locks require sixteen "units," so don't use them up doing laundry or taking on-shore showers. Buy another card if your need is greater.)

A note on currencies: Two currencies are used in Ireland: the British pound sterling (£) in Northern Ireland and the Irish pound or "punt" (IRE£) in the Republic. The former normally trades higher than the latter, somewhere in the vicinity of £1=US$1.5, while the punt runs around

IRE£1=US$1.20. Exchange rates can be found in most newspapers, or at banks, or at www.xe.net/currency. If traveling up or down the Shannon–Erne Link, there is never a problem exchanging £ sterling for IRE£ or vice versa.

Basic Planning

Planning your waterways adventure is dependent on which of the boating areas are of most interest. Each of the Shannon–Erne waterways chapters in this guide provides information on the physical character of the area and the boat rental system, adequate to help you make the best decisions and arrange the most rewarding journey. Each region requires some variation on the basic procedure of gathering boat rental company information, selecting your cruiser, determining the availability on the dates you want and, finally, booking and paying. But there is one early decision that is common to all: TIMING.

The most common rental period set by most boatyards is Saturday to Saturday, but as the number of travelers from overseas increases the companies are becoming more flexible. Thursday or Friday is not always the best day of the week in terms of transatlantic flights and fares, nor is it always the most convenient for vacationers who must take their time according to company calendars and schedules.

If a Saturday start day is a problem, several steps can be taken. First, try to avoid going in July or August, the months when most boatyards adhere more rigidly to the Saturday start dates. Second, check the websites or catalogs for those cruiser companies that have flexible days. During the months when there are fewer boaters, mid-week starts and three-day "short breaks" are available. This varies between boatyards, so select three or four suitable vessels and either fax, e-mail, or telephone the rental company stipulating your dates. This will work in the off-seasons, usually including the pleasant boating months of May, early June, and much of September.

If you are planning your trip for the period between mid-June and the first week of September, the months during which airfares as well as boat prices are highest, the best approach is to first arrange the best flight and best fare, then set your cruising period dates. Plan to arrive in Ireland a few days early, then take a hotel or B&B in the area of your selected boatyard. This makes your trip to the boatyard leisurely, allows time to get over jet lag, makes the Saturday start day feasible, and may save you money on the airfare.

International Air

The best destination airport or city in Ireland depends on what part of the lengthy Shannon–Erne system you want to explore, so the first step is to skip ahead in this guide, study the overviews and in-depth descriptions of the four sections of the system, decide where you want to cruise, then return to make the choice of destination airports and air carriers.

The best destination airport for boatyards of the Erne Lakes of Northern Ireland is Belfast, although most of the cruiser companies can also arrange transport through Dublin. The North Shannon, including the Ballinamore– Ballyconnell Link, is best served out of Dublin, although most cruiser companies also offer service from and to Belfast. The mid-Shannon riverports are equally well served out of Dublin and Shannon International Airport, while Shannon International is best for the boatyards of the South Shannon, including Lough Derg at the southern end and Lough Ree to its north.

We rarely recommend one airline over another, but when the service and comfort provided are exceptional we feel that there should be acknowledgement. Besides being the national airline of Ireland, Aer Lingus has for us consistently given such service in flights to both Shannon and Dublin.

Aer Lingus
Tel: 800-IRISH-AIR; Website: www.aerlingus.ie

Serves Shannon and Dublin International Airports from thirty cities in thirteen countries

Delta Airlines
Tel: 800-221-1212; Website: www.delta-air.com
Serves Belfast via British Airways Manchester

Continental Airlines
Tel: 800-231-0856; Website: www.flycontinental.com
Serves Shannon & Dublin International Airports direct from US and Canada

British Airways
Tel: 800-247-9297; Website: www.british-airways.com
Serves Belfast & Dublin direct, Shannon via Manchester

There are also other domestic flights between several airports in Britain and Belfast and international to Dublin and Shannon. The following additional airlines fly to London Heathrow and Gatwick (unless otherwise noted):

Virgin Atlantic Airlines
Tel: 800-862-8621; Website: www.fly.virgin.com/atlantic

United Airlines Tel: 800-241-6522; Website: www.ual.com
(Dublin & Belfast via London on British Midland)

TWA Tel: 800-221-2000; Website: www.twa.com
(Gatwick only)

Getting to & from the Boatyards

For travelers not renting a vehicle, transportation to and from the boatyards is arranged at the time of booking and is handled by either the cruiser company or an independent carrier that works with the cruiser companies. It's a very efficient and capable network. You will be instructed on this, but in general, transportation is simply a matter of being met at the airport baggage area, arrivals lounge, railway station, or ferryport by a driver who will know your name, your flight arrival information and to which community or boatyard you are to be taken. If you plan to arrive in the vicinity of your boatyard a day or more prior to the start date of your cruising, let the boat booking office know and they will arrange the pickup accordingly. If you plan to spend time in Dublin or Belfast before going to the boatyard, just tell the booking office what you want to do and they will let you know where and when the pickup will be made. Your return to the airport (or elsewhere) after cruising is arranged on your arrival at the boatyard.

Some of the carriers have regular schedules but with some flexibility if overseas travelers are arriving. The procedure is similar to arranging for a taxi or limousine pickup from home or a hotel to the airport.

Prices vary depending on the distance between the pickup point and the boatyard, but are on the order of about IRE£15–30 per person. Transit time between Shannon airport or Belfast or Dublin and Shannon river ports runs in the neighborhood of two hours.

An alternative is the public bus, a budget approach that will likely prove exhausting and difficult if attempted on the day of flight arrival. But if you plan to spend a night or more in Dublin or Belfast prior to departing for the marina, a bus is feasible.

More details on ground transportation are included in each of the later chapters, but if you are planning to travel independently by rail, for railway and ferry schedules purchase a Thomas Cook European Timetables or, for information and booking, contact:

Rail Pass Express
For rail passes & point-to-point ticket purchases:
Tel: 800-722-7151

Introduction

For point-to-point ticket information:
Tel: 614-793-7650 (9:00–3:00 EST M-F)
E-mail: relations@railpass.com; Website:www.railpass.com

Simply tell the operator your departure point and destination town (for example, London–Belfast via ferry) and the itinerary will be set up between the appropriate station, the intervening station if any, and the destination. Passes, rather than point-to-point, are appropriate for travelers planning rail excursions before or after cruising. Payment can be made by credit card.

Car rentals can be arranged through Hertz, Avis, and other major international rental companies. A substantial, and very good family-owned company with home offices in Knocklong, County Limerick, is Dan Dooley Rent-a-Car. The prices are competitive and there are seventeen offices throughout the Republic and Northern Ireland, including the major airports and ferryports.

In the US & Canada Tel: 800-331-9301
To Ireland Tel: 011-353-62-53103
E-mail: info@dan-dooley.ie
Website: www.dan-dooley.ie

Navigational Charts, Guides, & Environmental Information

Waterways are as scrupulously charted as any road map, and the charts are as easy to follow, perhaps more so because they are less complex. Moreover, the charts are often combined with detailed guides that provide not only full navigational information but locations and descriptions of all the boatyards in the area, small maps of town and other moorings, waterside inns, restaurants, pubs, footpaths, roads from the water's edge, special attractions. The Shannon–Erne Waterways Promotions, a public organization based in Ballinamore, has produced a very nice small guide that deals with details such as eating places as well as the history of places along the way. It is available at every boatyard and tourist office, and anything a boat traveler may need is included. These waterways have been plied for centuries, and many of them for pleasure alone for over a hundred years. A water-focused world exists and continues to grow, and there are many regional publications aimed at helping the traveler get the most enjoyment from it.

There are two sets of charts comprising two sections each for the River Shannon, and two sets of two charts each for the Shannon–Erne Link and the Erne. These are available at all the boatyards at a price of about US$12 per set. There are smaller charts in the Captain's Handbook provided by most of the cruiser companies, as well as reproductions in various regional guides, but we recommend buying the folding charts for their detail and ease of use.

Each of the following regional chapters characterizes the nature of the countryside through which the waterway passes in terms of towns and highlights, and an overview of the fauna and flora. Specific books on the subjects are also available, some through the boat rental companies, but many can be found in libraries and bookstores in the US. And we especially enjoyed having a good bird book along.

The excellent and detailed *Shell Guide to the River Shannon* is also available at bookstores and tourist offices in Ireland at about US$25.

Sample Itineraries

The number of possible starting and ending points from which to devise itineraries, plus the various amounts of time that boaters can allow for the voyages, combined with the parts of the waterway that appeal to some travelers and less so to others, (birds, fishing, towns, walks, historical sites, and so forth) make it hard to lay out the most desirable cruises for all boaters. Indeed, devising your own journey is part of the fun. There are many variations: Time may be spent fishing or not. Or more or less time spent in the villages, more or less on woodland walks, more or less engaged in photography, more or less on bird spotting. These then, are just a few ideas of how cruise itineraries can be put together. They reflect our leanings, drawn from our experience. The first description goes into detail in order to explain more or less what it's like.

South Shannon Round Trip (1 Week)

Arrive Shannon airport a day or two before cruise departure and travel to Killaloe (pronounced KILL-a-loo) where Ireland Line & Crown Blue Line have boatyards. Overnight at the Lakeside Hotel (100 yards from the marina). Dinner at Molly's Pub. If you haven't ordered groceries ahead, or need more, next day walk to Londis grocery (less than half a mile). They will deliver your bags to the boatyard. Visit the town, especially St. Flannan's Cathedral.

Day 1. Check in at Ireland Line Cruises; follow the instructional procedure. By the middle of the afternoon, load your luggage and groceries and depart upriver for a close-by overnight mooring, practicing boat operations on the way. Moor for the night at the village of Mountshannon.

Day 2. Detour south to cruise by Iniscealtra (Holy Island), then up the beautiful Scarriff River; return to the lake by early afternoon and cruise north to Portumna. Moor for the night.

Day 3. Check opening times of Portumna Bridge. Visit the town, the Portumna Priory, Castle Gordon; lunch at the Shannon Oaks hotel. Depart upriver. Moor for the night at Meelick Lock (2 hours) or Banagher town (3 hours).

Day 4. Depart upriver early: to Clonmacnois monastic ruins & museum (4 hours from Banagher). Allow 2–3 hours for Clonmacnois. Return downriver, overnight at Shannon Bridge (2 hours).

Day 5. Return to Lough Derg, pass Portumna, steer for

Terryglass for a visit (stop by the Old Church Gift Shop—as in all small private or community shops, there is no VAT [Value Added Tax] on purchases). Overnight here or return across lake to Portumna to explore the wild Portumna Forest Park.

Day 6. Cruise downlake, mooring at Dromineer for lunch at Dromineer Hotel and walk about the ruin and the ancient woolen mill. Cruise south for Garrykennedy mooring; small marina, tiny village, great traditional Irish music. If marina is full, allow for 1½-hour cruise time to moor at Killaloe.

Day 7. Return the cruiser by noon.

Alternative: There are two good cruiser bases, Waveline Cruisers at Killinure Point, and Lough Ree Cruisers at Mucknagh Point. Both are near Glasson on the Inner Loughs at the southeast end of Lough Ree. Good round-trip itineraries can be planned either uplake or downriver.

South–North Shannon Linear (1 Week)

Although this brief illustration is laid out from south to north, like any one-way itinerary it can be taken in either direction. Arrive Shannon airport and travel to Portumna OR arrive Dublin and travel to Banagher. The illustration will take us from the southernmost. Important note: The only boat companies with two bases for one-way itineraries on the Shannon are Emerald Star-Connoisseur and Carrick Craft.

Day 1. Depart Portumna (Connaught Harbor) southbound into Lough Derg. Moor at Portumna; visit Portumna Priory, Castle Gordon, and Forest Park OR moor across the lake at Terryglass. (Similar itinerary from Banagher—a bit upriver.)

Day 2. Cruise south to Mountshannon for overnight mooring (6 hours).

Day 3. Return northward and overnight at either Terryglass or Portumna, visiting Dromineer en route.

Day 4. Cruise upriver through Meelick Lock; visit Banagher. Continue to Shannon Bridge for the night mooring. (From Portumna 6 hours).

Introduction

Day 5. Depart upriver early: to Clonmacnois monastic ruins & museum (1 hour from Shannon Bridge). Allow 2–3 hours for Clonmacnois. Depart upriver by early afternoon, past Athlone (1 hour), on into Lough Ree and into Hodson Bay for the night (elegant restaurant and a good pub at Hodson Bay Hotel 100 yards from the marina).

Day 6. Depart uplake; 7 hours cruising to night mooring at Dromod Harbor, stopping by Roosky en route.

Day 7. Cruise Dromod to Carrick-on-Shannon (3 hours). Return cruiser by noon.

Shannon South–North Linear Alternative #1: The upper reaches of Lough Derg are an important and unusual bird sanctuary whose marshes and fen are difficult to visit except by boat. Portumna Forest Park is also extensive and rich in wildlife. Spend more time in that area and forego the round-trip cruise as far south as Mountshannon.

Shannon South–North Linear Alternative #2: Forego Lough Derg and the river south of Banagher. Start at Banagher, cruise north to first night at Shannon Bridge; Day 2 visit Clonmacnois, then Athlone for the night. Day 3 visit Athlone town and the castle, then cruise eastward to explore the beautiful "inner lakes" and overnight at the public Ballykeeran Marina; day 4 uplake 7 hours cruising to Dromod Harbor; day 5 upriver past Carrick-on-Shannon into the River Boyle mooring at Coothall. Day 6 into Lough Key; moor and spend time at Lough Key Forest Park and town of Boyle; day 7 return downriver to Carrick-on-Shannon and return cruiser.

North Shannon–Link–Erne Linear Cruise

To illustrate another one-way option, for our first cruise on the Ireland waterway we came into Dublin, took the Shannon–Erne mini-bus to Carrick-on-Shannon, spent the night at the Bush Hotel, then took a cruiser northward into Lough Key (day 1) where we moored for the night, returned to the Shannon, turned northward again and followed the Shannon–Erne Link (days 2 and 3) into the Erne lake system. That gave us the four remaining days of our week to cruise the Erne lakes as far as Inishmacsaint Island west of Enniskillen before backtracking uplake to return the boat to the northern base at Belturbet on the upper River Erne.

Either direction is fine. For example, Erincurrach Cruising, Carrick Craft, and Emerald Star-Connoisseur make possible interesting one-way itineraries in which most of the time is spent on the Erne Lakes, then traveling southbound to their bases in the River Boyle near Coothall (Erincurrach) on the south end or at Carrick-on-Shannon.

Two-Week Linear Cruise

Again, the direction of travel is immaterial; it may be set more by the best airfares between North America and either Belfast, Dublin, or Shannon. Indeed, the best arrangement might be open jaw tickets—into Shannon and out of Dublin, for example. For Dublin arrivals, the closest of the southern dual-base boatyards is at Banagher (Carrick Craft), from where a short trip south for a glimpse of Lough Derg (6–7 hours round trip) can be accomplished before heading north for two weeks toward Carrick-on-Shannon, through the Link and around the Erne Lakes to the drop-off at Knockninny Quay near Enniskillen, and a return to either Dublin or Belfast.

For arrivals at Shannon, the closest boatbase of companies that have two or more bases is at Portumna (Emerald Star-Connoisseur). From Portumna, a leisurely week long cruise to Carrick-on-Shannon is easy, and two weeks on through the Link into and through the Erne lakes with the drop-off at Belturbet and return to Dublin is ideal, and even allows a day for cruising northern Lough Derg before departing northward.

Erne Round Trips

A delightfully full week can also be spent on the Erne lakes, picking up a cruiser at any of the single-boatyard or dual-boatyard companies and returning it to the point of origin, never having left the lake and river system. This is an excellent idea for anyone especially interested in visiting outstanding ruins of sixth- through ninth-century monastic settlements, walking through the nature preserve at Crom estate, mooring on wooded islands, visiting Belleek and the Belleek Pottery plant, exploring Enniskillen and the castle, and going to nearby stately houses such as the National Trust's Castle Coole and Florence Court, or the nearby Marble Arch Caves, one of the finest show caves of Europe.

These are only a few of many possible versions that can be planned and carried out, some of which might be determined by your point of entry into Ireland: Shannon, Dublin or Belfast by air (or possibly Rosslare Harbour, Dublin/Dun Laoghaire, Belfast, or Larne by ferry from Britain). This decision on destination may, in turn, be dependent on the best airfare or schedule from North America.

Waterside Support

Boatyards, or boatbases, can be likened to a combination of a land-based service station and car rental office. The motor cruisers are always checked out, clean, fueled and ready to go. The boatyards of the Shannon–Erne are not far from one another, so assistance is readily available, and even in the most isolated parts of the river or lakes there are other boaters to lend a hand. Nevertheless, boaters should plan to end the daily travel by late afternoon or early evening. For the utmost sense of security, cell phones are increasingly available for rent.

Because many travelers from overseas may not choose to rent a car, each chapter of the guide contains recommendations and profiles on the best and most convenient pickup and drop-off boatyards accessible by rail, bus, minibus, and taxi. Each "Captain's Handbook" contains complete information on actions to be taken in case of emergency or for any need of assistance such as non-emergency failure of the refrigerator, cabin heater, TV, engine, and the like. Every member of the hire boat associations in Ireland and Britain is pledged to assist any boater with problems or in trouble, thus creating a network of boater support throughout the waterways systems. Telephone numbers are provided in order to call the boatyard; distress flags are provided, to be flown if necessary so that any boater will come to your aid.

Provisioning: The Essentials

Provisioning is like shopping anywhere. Before departure it is simply a matter of going to the nearest grocery store to buy food and other basics for a couple of days. Ask at the rental office about what supplies, if any, are provided, because this varies among the boat companies. For coffee drinkers, the item we most often found missing was a coffee maker or even cone-type filter. And we rarely found those most useful supplies such as liquid soap, salt, pepper, sugar, paper towels, paper napkins, zip-lock bags, and hand soap. If not already supplied, buy what is needed, including (for coffee drinkers) a small plastic filter cone holder, or one of the neat collapsible net filters that we have found only in the UK and Ireland.

There are refrigerators on all the boats, but the freezers are usually small. There is no need to buy food for the week because it's easy (by following the site-specific charts), to tie up at some town quay along the water and do the shopping in the village. We leaned toward prepared foods, of which Irish markets, even the small 24-hour type like our 7-11, offer an abundance, ranging from all sorts of pot pies, meat and vegetable pasties, quiches, curries, deli salads, and, of course, pizzas. Many small grocery stores thrive on cruising clientele, so there is no absence of any kind of food, except perhaps Mexican.

Introduction

Many boat companies send with the booking form a grocery-shopping list; order ahead and it will be delivered to your boat when you arrive. If there is no list and you want to order in advance, just ask the boat company if they will place an order, then draw up a list and send it. There is rarely a delivery fee—the order is simply placed with the nearby local grocer who does the shopping for you and takes it to the boatyard. It's a good way to start, even if it's just for the basic supplies mentioned above plus coffee, tea, milk, bread, breakfast items, fruit, and perhaps something frozen for the first night out.

For any marina where grocery buying is awkward or difficult, the cruiser line profiles in the regional chapters contain details on how to handle the situation.

Rent-a-Dinghy & Rent-a-Bicycle

Although most cruisers include a dinghy in the rent, a few may charge a modest amount (around US$60 per week). In any case it's a good idea to take one for the added convenience as well as the sense of safety in case of the unlikely event of grounding or a loss of power. There are also many times when one of these small boats come in handy, such as for fishing, for venturing for a short distance into a canal or small estuary where your larger boat cannot venture, or for going ashore from your boat if it is anchored or tied up away from the dock or jetty.

Bicycles are available for rent, or can be arranged for, at most boatyards, and taken on board. They are modestly priced and enable travelers to explore the waterside paths, fens, and forests as well as make greater distances through towns.

The Boat & Cottage Option

In the preface we described our first contact with the world of rental boats, describing our stay in a modern townhouse facing a strip of grass and a row of small trees bordering a concrete quay. In fact, the townhouse we were renting was one of literally hundreds of "cottages" available throughout Great Britain for short-term vacation rent from Blakes, the same company that rents boats. Although it is no longer in the cottage rental business, the other large boat rental company, Hoseasons, remains a cottage rental organization.

We have long been champions of settling in for a week or two when visiting Europe. Staying in a vacation rental, whether it is an apartment in London or Venice, a farmhouse in Provence, or a chalet in the Alps, immerses one in the local culture, and not only provides more space for less money, but also a sense of being part of the community rather than just a tourist. This approach to visiting Europe seems to combine nicely with the idea of renting a boat. A week exploring by waterway coupled with a week or so in a rental cottage or apartment is ideal. Renting a land-bound accommodation is as easy as renting a boat, with much of the same planning devoted to choosing a location. There are always cottage rentals available in the vicinity of the Shannon and its lakes and bays, and along the Erne. The best approach once a decision has been made on location is to contact one of the rental agents (see Appendix 3).

CHAPTER 2

Erne Lakes and the River Erne: Belleek to Crom Castle & Belturbet

The Erne Lakes and river are the farthest northern part of the unified Shannon–Erne Waterway. Most of this section lies in Northern Ireland, County Fermanagh (pronounced fer-MAN-ahg), where the currency is £ sterling rather than IRE£, as it is in the Republic. They say, though, that at Belleek you can stand in the water of the Erne in the UK and catch a salmon in the Republic. And the source of the River Erne lies in the hills of the Republic's County Cavan, as does Belturbet, a main town and marina of the Shannon–Erne system.

We first came into Upper Lough Erne in 1996 from the south, by way of a rented cabin cruiser out of Carrick-on-Shannon. From the Shannon headwaters near Carrick we cruised up the Shannon–Erne Link, then better known as the Ballinamore–Ballyconnell Canal, to the high point of the watershed, then down the canal and Woodford River into the Erne. The Woodford flows into the River Erne just as the Erne broadens to become Upper Lough Erne. It was late afternoon, and to our left on a tiny wooded island rose a gray crenellated tower. To our right, on a distant forested shore stood a ruin that our chart told us was Castle Crom. We looked westerly, toward the more than 300 square miles of unspoiled waterways that lace County Fermanagh, Ulster's Lake District, dominated by the slender, island-filled upper lake and broad Lower Lough Erne between Belturbet and Belleek.

The Erne Countryside

The Erne waterway begins in the hills of County Cavan, from which the River Erne flows northwesterly on its journey to Donegal Bay and the Atlantic. The linear distance is only 60 miles or so by the most direct route, or it can be turned into 100 or more miles by boaters who want to visit coves and inlets, circle islands and divert themselves into marinas and other moorings along the way. Just west (downriver) of the headwater end of navigation near the town of Belturbet, the Erne widens and creates two lakes, Upper and Lower Lough Erne, the first narrow and island-dotted, the lower lake broadening beyond Enniskillen to vast open water.

The countryside is rural, forested and hilly, the south river and lake bank sloping upward toward the Northern Ireland–Republic political border and the watershed divide along the highest range. Beyond the northerly shores, gentler hills and meadowlands shape the land. It is an area of supreme and tranquil beauty, where the signs of early human intrusions actually enhance the interest, and carry the mind back to the distant past.

Between the two lakes the waterway again becomes the river, forming an hourglass shape at whose narrow part sits the small city of Enniskillen. The first view to boaters traveling downstream is the impregnable-looking, yet somehow benign, Enniskillen castle rising on the riverbanks. A few miles beyond the narrows the water broadens again and encompasses a number of islands, of which some are among the most remarkable and treasured remnants of monastic communities in Ireland and Europe (see the following section).

Downlake beyond where the ruins of Castle Tully stand on clifftop, Lower Lough Erne is expansive open water, dominated by the sheer and imposing Cliffs of Magho on the south bank. At its lower end the lake is separated by a forested peninsula; to its north a narrow bay leads to the mooring at Castle Caldwell and to the south it becomes the river again, with a more or less straight course for three miles to the end of cruiser navigation at the town of Belleek and, six miles beyond that, Donegal Bay and the Atlantic.

Towns & Highlights

The following highlights are all easy to locate on the chart of the Erne Waterway. The three main towns along the Erne waterway are Belturbet (on the river at the upper end of navigation), Enniskillen (at the narrows between the upper and lower lakes), and Belleek (at the lower end of navigation). For boaters, all are sources of supplies, and for everyone, all are worth a visit.

Between the towns are many moorings, some in isolated bays, some in marinas, as well as numerous points of importance, which are indeed a main reason for exploring the Erne. All are worth a stop. These highlights follow in order from the river headwaters northwestward and down-lake toward the sea. Unless otherwise noted, there are moorings at these points.

Belturbet, in County Cavan of the Republic, is not a complex little town, but the river adds to its pleasant character, and it is the north marina for the hire boat company Emerald Star-Connoisseur Cruisers (other marinas are at Carrick-on-Shannon and Portumna far to the south; see profile in this chapter). There are grocery stores within easy walking distance of the marina.

Crom Estate & Castle lie along the water's edge where the river broadens into Upper Lough Erne, about an hour cruising downriver from Belturbet. The early seventeenth-century castle stands as a dramatic ruin near the shore, while in the near distance the large nineteenth-century manor house remains the home of the Earls of Erne. The 3,500-acre **Crom Estate and Nature Conservation** has recently been turned over by the Earl to the National Trust, and is a delight to visit, from the paths through the woods to the Trust's visitor center.

Cottages are also available for rent there from the National Trust (Tel: 011-44-28-6773-8118 or Central Reservations in England: Tel: 011-44-1225-791199). The wildness of the reed marshes, fens, forests, castle, and myriad water birds lured us to spend the night at the mooring near the ruin. It is one of Ireland's most important nature conservation areas and is of international significance.

The medieval **Enniskillen Castle** rises from the river and dominates the water approach to the city from the east; it houses two interesting museums, the **Fermanagh County Museum** and the **Museum of the Inniskilling Fusiliers**, both providing good perspectives on the history of the area. Enniskillen is the commercial and cultural center of the area as well as the county seat of Fermanagh. A modern shopping mall contrasts with the buildings of the old city, but is easily accessible to the public moorings at the **Lakeland Forum** just below the castle. The Lakeland Forum is open to the public for swimming, showers, and the like. There are good pubs and restaurants within an easy walk from the public moorings.

Enniskillen Castle, County Fermanagh, from the River Erne

The Lakeland mooring is the closest to the city center, the Henry Street mooring is across the river above the bridge, and a very nice one called Round O Jetty, is alongside a park 200 yards below the bridge. Another mooring, Riverview Jetty, lies along the north side of the island on which most of Enniskillen lies, and yet another is just below the **Ardhowen Arts Centre** with a bar, restaurant, theater, and concert hall.

An important side trip, very well worth the bus or taxi ride, is the National Trust's **Castle Coole** on the outskirts of Enniskillen. It is one of the best examples of neo-classical buildings in the British Isles, an immense and magnificent house of almost palatial proportions in terms of size and the beauty of its furnishings. Built in the early 1800s, Castle Coole represents the highest expression of the work of architect James Wyatt. The elegant and clean design sitting somewhat aloof in the uncluttered landscape dominates the surrounding open fields for some distance. There are numerous service quarters to be visited, including a servants' tunnel, laundry house, dairy, and ice house. Although there is no special formal garden, there is a surrounding wooded landscape park.

The other nearby National Trust property, **Florence Court**, some dozen miles from Enniskillen, is one of Ulster's most important houses, built in the mid-eighteenth-century by John Cole, father of the first Earl of Enniskillen, and famous for its rococo plasterwork and fine pieces of Irish furniture. Interesting service quarters surround cobbled courtyards. There is a water-powered sawmill, a walled garden, ice house, and spectacular views. The magnificent park contains many notable mature trees. Check with the tourist office at Enniskillen (100 yards from the mooring upstream of the castle) for local bus information. The following list of hotels in Enniskillen may be helpful: (Tel: 011-44-)

The Killyhevlin Hotel***: Dublin Road.
Tel: 2866-323481; Fax: 2866-324726
Belmore Court Motel**: Tempo Road.
Tel: 2866-326633; Fax: 2866-326362

E-mail: Belmore@travel-ireland.com

Fort Lodge Hotel**: 72 Forthill Street.
   Tel: 2866-323275; Fax: 2866-323275

Railway Hotel*: 34 Forthill Street.
   Tel: 2866-322084; Fax: 2866-327480

Manor House Country Hotel***: Killadeas, 10 miles up
   the north shore from Enniskillen.
   Tel: 2866-621561; Fax: 2866-621545

Lower Lough Erne especially abounds in prominent sites dating from the early centuries of Christianity in Ireland. The island of **Devenish** (pronounced Daimh-inis), just twenty minutes downlake of Enniskillen, is one of the best of these ancient monastic gems. From the jetty one looks up the hill toward the remains of tiny twelfth-century **St. Molaise's House**, and on to the imposing stone Round Tower, its point piercing the sky some eighty feet above its base. Founded at the height of the monastic period in Ireland in the early sixth century, Devenish flourished until a waterborne Viking attack in 837 made evident the vulnerability of the settlements of the Erne. In the ninth and tenth century, round towers served as the early warning system, built for sounding the alarm upon spotting intruders, and for storing sacred and other vital documents. The Devenish round tower is one of the finest remaining in Ireland.

The origins of the church ruin on nearby **White Island** are obscure, but it is the strange stone figures that are truly a mystery. The round eyes stare forward under the heavy brows of outsized heads. Perhaps revered at some ancient point in time, they became only building blocks for the Romanesque church that succeeded whatever it was that had first housed the figures. (The Aghinver Boat marina is located just across a narrow channel from White Island and Castle Archdale marina is a few hundred yards to the south.)

Not as imposing as the Devenish community, the tiny sixth-century church and great high cross on the island of

View of Round Tower toward jetty, Lower Lake Erne, Devenish

Inishmacsaint, 2 hours downlake of Devenish, are nevertheless an important stop. The founding saint, Ninnid, was a contemporary of Molaise of Devenish and of Ciarán, who began the great monastic community of Clonmacnois along the River Shannon far to the south.

Given to him by the crown after it seized Irish lands in 1607, Sir John Hume of Berwickshire had **Tully Castle** built in 1613. In 1641 Rory McGuire, returning to recapture his family lands, killed most of the occupants and burned the castle. Hume never returned, but the stone walls remain standing high on a cliff overlooking the lake and the mooring at Sand Bay, a brooding testament to a tragic history. Just east of the Tully Castle mooring is the full service marina of Erincurrach Cruising.

Down the broad lake from Tully Castle, the peninsula that juts into the lake upriver from Belleek is a nature reserve. On the north side lies a bay ending at a jetty near the ruins of **Castle Caldwell.** Along the forested shoreline of the bay grow rare fen and marsh plants. Nature trails accessible from the mooring run along the sides of the peninsula, and the area is a nesting place for sparrowhawks and crossbill.

Belleek is a quaint village filled with shops, traditional pubs, and tourist attractions, the most important being the factory and factory store of **Belleek Pottery Ltd.**, home of world famous Belleek china and porcelain. There is good mooring there and the boatyard of the community's rental cruiser company, Belleek Charter Cruising (see profile in this chapter).

Flora & Wildlife

Unlike the broad low meadows and extensive marshlands of the central and lower Shannon, the borders of the Erne rise more abruptly to hills and slopes and are more forested with deciduous trees. Thus, although there are many, many plant species, the habitat is less varied and smaller in scope than that associated with the Shannon. Nevertheless, the reedy and marshy verges of the upper end of Upper Lough Erne and the meanders of the river up to Belturbet are home to orchids, water plantain, sedges, flowering rush, and such delicate plants as ragged robin and the more rare marsh pea.

As along the Woodford River end of the Shannon–Erne Link, swans, gray herons, great crested grebes, mallards, and teal are the predominant birdlife of the waterways. We had heard that the verges of the island channels of Upper Lough Erne are the nesting area for more than five percent of the world's whooper swans, and by the time we had cruised into Enniskillen we felt that we'd seen most of them.

Overall, Upper Lough Erne is considered one of Ireland's most important bird areas. The many islands, bays, forested shores, edge marshes, and strangely isolated character make it home to a considerable variety of species. An ancient oak forest on Inishfendra, an island off the Crom Estate at the upper end of Upper Lough Erne, just across the narrows of upper Lough Erne where the Woodford flows into the lake, is the largest heronry in Ireland. There, at the National Trust office, we asked about a large ferret-like creature we'd spotted during our walk in the woods and were told that we'd seen a pine marten. They are reclusive, but since the area became protected their number has grown and they have become a menace to the eggs of the heronry, much to the distress of the herons and heron lovers. More study is now needed.

Kestrel and sparrowhawks nest and live in another oakwood just across the lake near the end of a narrow bay leading to Teemore. In the winter near the north shore village of Linaskea you may spot snipe and water rail; in the summer you will find lapwing and redshank instead. We never spotted a cuckoo, but in the evening we heard their cries.

The primary appeal of the Erne waterway is its all-encompassing natural quality, its very active birdlife, its variety of the flora, the juxtaposition of lakes, inlets and countryside, of water and forests—not to mention the many evidences of an ancient and civilized past.

Fish & Fishing

In late May mornings the parking lot near the tourist center in Enniskillen fills with anglers gathering for the Fermanagh (County) Classic Fishing Festival, but within an hour the lot is empty, the length and breadth of the rivers and lakes having absorbed them all. There is a spring salmon run, trout in the lakes and the river, and large pike can be taken where fodder fish provide their food in the two large lakes. The specimen pike (20 pounds for the river, 30 pounds for the lakes) are not as common here as on the large lakes of the Shannon, so if this is the aim of a trip to Ireland, the chances are a bit better in Lough Derg, Ree, and Allen to the south.

Along the banks of the entire waterway anglers sit on shore or in hire cruisers aiming for coarse fish, principally roach, bream, and rudd. Serious anglers, especially from Britain and the Continent, make their headquarters at the **International Fishing Centre** near Belturbet. Licenses are required for salmon and trout, but not for coarse fishing. For more information, contact the Northern Ireland Tourist Board in New York or the Fermanagh Tourist Information Centre Tel: 011-44-2866-323110; Fax: 325511.

Navigation

The entire Erne system has been very well marked, and the markings and surveys translated into good charts for boaters. In addition to the Captain's Handbook given by the hire boat companies, the Erne Charter Association has produced a folding chart that we recommend. It shows all navigation markers, shallows, islands, rocks, jetties, moorings, and on-shore facilities, including fueling and water points, grocery stores, pubs, and waterside restaurants.

The Navigation Markers are large and easily visible signs installed along the waterway to tell boaters where the water is sufficiently deep for passage, or where it is not, and warn where there may be other dangers such as submerged rocks. In the Erne system the large round markers are placed either on buoys or at the tops of poles driven into the river or lake bottom. One side of the disk is painted white and faces toward the safe water channel, so the key is simply to keep the boat between those white sides and away from the other side, which is painted red. In narrow waters the markers come in pairs, easy to spot. In broader waters there may be a marker or series of markers on one side only, designating a shallow bay or submerged rocks; steer to the white side. The markers are also numbered, so it's easy to know precisely where you are simply by noting the coinciding number on the chart.

Navigation is easy on the Erne, but it's important to refer to the chart often and to keep alert to your position. The most common error made by boaters is failing to accurately locate the cruiser on the chart and entering a shallow bay or cove. At times, too, it may be difficult spot markers in the dusk or poor weather. Good compact binoculars are a definite help.

Cruising Times

With all the sites to stop by, the towns to explore, the monastic ruins to visit, the forest walks to take, the pubs and restaurants to enjoy, the pauses for photography, the picnics, figure a week for a round trip from any starting-returning point. If planning a single starting and ending boatyard, we recommend making better time going, saving time to return to places and sites you noticed outbound. In this way of pacing yourself, you won't need to worry about missing a particular site because of a final rush to return the boat. Plan to spend the last night moored within a few hours of your home base.

Assuming no stops and maximum cruising speed, the following are the approximate one-way cruise times in hours between key points in the Erne Lakes/Erne River waterway, into the Shannon–Erne Link and northern Shannon marinas. The two south Shannon towns are shown for illustration. Shannon River times are shown in the Shannon sections of this chapter. (See Appendix for Average Cruising Times for the entire waterway system.)

Belturbet to Crom Castle	1 hour
Belturbet to Enniskillen	5 hours
Belturbet to Belleek	9 hours
Belturbet to Corraquill (Lock No. 1)	2 hours
Belturbet to Carrick-on-Shannon (Emerald Star-Connoisseur bases)	16 hours
Enniskillen to Devenish	1 hour
Enniskillen to Inishmacsaint	2 hours
Belleek to Corraquill (Lock No. 1)	10 hours
Belleek to Ballyconnell (Link)	13 hours
Belleek to Ballinamore (Link)	16 hours
Blaney* to Coothall (Boyle/Shannon) (Erincurrach/Shannon–Erne bases)	4 hours
Knockninny* to Carrick-on-Shannon (Carrick Craft bases)	20 hours

Belturbet to Portumna (S. Shannon)	35 hours
(Emerald Star-Connoisseur bases)	
Knockninny to Banagher (S. Shannon)	37 hours
(Carrick Craft bases)	

* Blaney is approximately 9 miles west of Enniskillen along the south shore of Lower Lough Erne, and Knockninny is about 10 miles east of Enniskillen on the south shore of Upper Lough Erne.

BOAT RENTAL COMPANIES & BASES

All the cruiser rental companies of the Erne have a variety of boats available to choose from, some new, some older, but all we saw in boatyards and moorings along the way appeared to be well maintained. The competition is keen. Most are small to midsize family-owned and operated companies (Erincurrach Cruising, Lochside Cruisers, Manor House Marine, Erne Marine, Carrybridge Boat Company, Aghinver Boat Company), two are large (Carrick Craft and Emerald Star-Connoisseur), and one is run by the community (Belleek Charter Cruising).

Three of the nine companies have more than one boatyard, allowing (but not limited to) one-way trips, while the others specialize in the Erne waterway system and in itineraries south through the canal that of course must be repeated north-bound to return to the starting boat base.

For visitors who choose to rent a car, no points in the Erne waterways are so distant from Belfast or even Dublin that driving to them is inconvenient. (It's only 85 miles from Belfast to Enniskillen, half again that from Dublin).

Travelers without a rental vehicle should in almost all cases take advantage of the bus or mini-bus service offered by the boat companies. They are usually transportation companies not unlike those that provide shuttle or limousine service to and from airports in the US, Canada, and elsewhere. There is a flat fee (noted in the following profiles), and the pickup places and times are arranged during the process of booking.

Boaters planning *one-way voyages* of one week duration between northern and southern boat bases through the locks, loughs, and rivers of the Shannon–Erne need to book with Carrick Craft, Emerald Star-Connoisseur or Erincurrach Cruising. One-way between Belleek and Carrick-on-Shannon in the south can be arranged with Belleek Charter Cruising in off seasons. Anyone planning extensive one-way voyages of more than one week duration between northern and southern boat bases need to book with Carrick Craft or Emerald Star-Connoisseur whose bases are at the extreme ends. Anticipate a surcharge (drop-off) for one-way itineraries with the boat companies that have bases in more than one location. The amounts are shown where applicable.

Security deposits are required by all the hire boat companies, ranging between £150 and £350 depending on the size of the vessel. This refundable deposit can be made by credit car, with the charge simply not recorded unless the boat is returned damaged. An option is to purchase damage insurance.

Getting to the Boatyards

Transportation from and to Belfast and Dublin can be arranged through all the hire boat companies. This is usually by means of a van, minibus, or coach that collects clients at the terminals of the principal airports and ferryports. All flight arrival information must be given to the boat company, which, in turn, schedules the pickups at the appropriate arrivals lounge or baggage area. Cost of one-way transportation runs from about £15 to £20 per person, double that for round trip (called "return" by the British and Irish). This is the typical, and best, transportation for travelers without a vehicle. Unless otherwise noted, this means of transfer is available from the cruiser companies.

Public transportation is possible to a few of the boatyards

and is noted in the profiles as applicable. There are three to five departures daily by public bus (Bus Éirean) between Dublin (Busaras station) and Enniskillen, a 3-hour trip for about £9 one-way. En route is the town of Cavan, from which a taxi can be taken to Belturbet (Emerald Star-Connoisseur Cruisers boatyard) for about £8.

There is also bus service between Belfast central and Enniskillen (2+ hours) for about £7. We found the bus service to be very good, speedy, and comfortable. Taxi prices from Enniskillen to nearby boatyards are shown in the boat company profiles.

Be alert to the cruising start days of the company you book with, and even to the start days of particular cruisers. Saturdays are the norm, but more and more companies are adding other days of the week, most often giving a choice between Wednesday, Friday, and Saturday.

The approach we recommend, when flexible trip scheduling is possible, is to plan to arrive in your airport destination city a day or two ahead of the cruising start day. Arrange in advance with the boat company your transportation for that day, then book a hotel in Enniskillen, Belturbet, or Killadeas, or a B&B near the boatyard (arranged by the boat company), for a night to orient yourselves and get over jet lag, then take a taxi to the boatyard the following day. There is plenty to do and see in Enniskillen to occupy the time.

Cruiser Line Profiles

Note: Fermanagh County (UK) telephone country code is international access +44; all others are in the Republic, code +353. From the US and Canada, access is 011.

• Belleek Charter Cruising
Base: Belleek (Extreme West Lough Erne)
Corry, Belleek
Co. Fermanagh, BT93 3FU

No. Ireland
Tel: 44-2868-658027; Fax: 44-2868-658793
E-mail: belleektrust@btinternet.com
Website: www.angelfire.com/co/belleekcruising

This is an unusual hire boat company in that it is owned and operated by the community of Belleek for the improvement and enhancement of the town. The directors are unpaid, and all net profits are put back into the company and its community holdings.

The small marina sits next to the tourist information center just a few hundred yards from the plant, kilns, and museum of the famed Belleek Pottery, itself just at the start of the main street. This point on the River Erne, not far from the Atlantic, is the end of navigation (or the beginning) of the waterway that stretches for nearly 300 miles, first eastward up the Lower and Upper Erne lakes, then southwest up the Woodford River into the Shannon–Erne Link and the Republic of Ireland, then downward and southward on the River Shannon toward Carrick, Athlone, and the towns of Killaloe and Limerick.

There are only twelve cruisers in the fleet, and two sizes, the 36-ft. Wave Runner and the 38-ft. Morrell, sleeping 4+2 and 6+2 respectively. These are very heavy steel hull cruisers, 9 tons and 14 tons, one of only two companies that have such boats (Tara Cruisers in Lough Key off the Shannon is the other). Accordingly, they have bow thrusters operated from the flybridge by push button in order to make steering when mooring agile and responsive. They are comfortably designed for inside living, all have two helm positions, diesel-fired heating, handrails all around, depth finders, and two toilet/shower rooms.

The location of the marina makes it especially ideal for boaters who like the broad waters of large lakes such as lower Lough Erne as well as lock-free cruising in the smaller upper lake with its complex shoreline and many islands.

Transportation can be arranged from Dublin and Belfast to either Belleek or Ballinamore for about £30 per person round trip. For boaters with cars, parking is available near both the Belleek and Ballinamore moorings.

Rates are very good for cruisers of this size, running from about £740 per week for the 4+2 berth in low season to £1,200 for the 38-foot 6+2 berth.

If departing from the boatyard at mid-afternoon, there is a public marina at the west end of town ten minutes away, or a good first night around the nature reserve peninsula at the Castle Caldwell jetty. One way itineraries between Belleek and Carrick-on-Shannon south of the Link may be assanged in low season.

• Erincurrach Cruising

Other Base: Knockvicar on River Boyle (North Shannon)
Assoc. with Shannon Erne Waterway Holidays Ltd.
Blaney, Enniskillen,
Co. Fermanagh, BT93 7EQ
No. Ireland
Tel: 44-2868-641507; Fax: 44-2868-641734
E-mail: helen@irelandboating.com
Website: www.irelandboating.com
Shannon Base Tel: 353-79-67028; Fax: 353-79-67333
E-mail: sewh@tinet.ie
Website: www.sew-holidays.com
Agents: UK: Blakes Holiday Boating; US: Great Trips Unlimited, Blakes Vacations (see Appendix)

Located at Blaney on the south shore of Lower Lough Erne (12 miles from Enniskillen), the company has been operating as Erincurrach Cruising for about eleven years from a single base primarily serving the Erne Lakes, where it still specializes. It has now set up a link and formed an association with Shannon Erne Waterway Holidays Ltd. at a base south of the Shannon–Erne Link in order to offer one-way trips in either direction. This provides an excellent span, ideal for one-week one-way itineraries.

There are about twenty-four cruisers in all, of which thirteen are normally in Blaney and eleven in Coothall. Of these, more than half are newer than three years old. The fleet consists of all types/sizes, sleeping from two to six persons, of which only the Devenish (2+2 berths) and Tully (6+2 berths) are available for the one-way bookings. We see this as no problem. Prices range from about £495 per week in low season for the smallest cruiser to £1,250 for the 6+2 berth Tully in peak season.

Transportation: Friday and Saturday start days are offered, and transport from and to Belfast (£32 per person round trip) and Dublin (£36) can be arranged at time of booking. Pick up days are Wednesday, Friday, and Saturday. There are also three to five departures daily by Bus Éirean between Dublin (Busaras station) and Donegal (Abbey Hotel); the fare is about £9 one-way. Ticket yourself only to Blaney and remind the driver—you will be let off within 100 yards of the boatyard reception building. As noted above, bus service also runs between Belfast and Enniskillen.

There are B&B's in the vicinity and accommodation can be arranged for at the time of booking for anyone who wants a rest night before departing by boat. The company will transport clients. Or take an Enniskillen hotel (see Towns & Highlights earlier in chapter). Taxi fare from Enniskillen to Blaney is about £8.

Provisioning: Because the boatbase is not in a town, a grocery order form is sent to clients by mail or fax. We suggest ordering sufficient for several meals, then cruising into Enniskillen or Belleek at your leisure to moor and buy more groceries.

We recommend Erincurrach Cruising as an attractive and well-maintained fleet; we liked all the cruisers. The reception room shows the same care, and the self-catering cottages are impeccable. Bicycles are available for rent, as well as fishing gear.

There are several quiet moorings nearby for the first night out: Tully Castle is only fifteen minutes, Inishmacsaint a half an hour or, across the lake, at Rossigh or Rossclare Bay.

The relatively small size allows for personal attention of the owners/management, Charlie and Helen Parke; coupled with an attractive marina near midway between the interesting and desirable towns of Belleek and Enniskillen, this makes for a very nice boat company to work with. Also, there are two rows of modern vacation rental cottages overlooking Lough Erne and the marina, each rental including a small boat with outboard, ideal for nearby exploring and fishing.

Book with the Blaney headquarters or, if planning a one-way trip, either here or with the southern marina located near Knockvicar/Coothall on the River Boyle, just upriver from its confluence with the Shannon near Carrick-on-Shannon.

For river and lake details near the southern base see the Shannon–Erne Waterway Holidays profile in Chapter 5.

• Lochside Cruisers
Base: Enniskillen (Mid-Erne)
Tempo Road, Enniskillen,
Co. Fermanagh, BT74 6HR
No. Ireland
Tel: 44-2866-324368; Fax: 44-2866-325209
E-mail: boats@lochside.ie
Website: www.lochside.ie
Agents: UK: Blakes Holiday Boating; US: Great Trips Unlimited, Blakes Vacations (see Appendix)

The affable Des Dolan and his family have owned and operated this relatively small fleet for some twenty-seven years, specializing on the Erne waters. From their boatyard about half a mile from the bridge in central Enniskillen, the upper and lower lakes form a figure eight, with Lochside at the narrow point. And the figure eight is the best way to plan an itinerary, starting either uplake or down. (Unless you've placed an advance grocery order, the first stop would be across the river to the Lakeland Center mooring near the shopping center.)

The nineteen cruisers are distinctive not only in their red, white, and pale blue coloring, but in their rather unconventional, yet handsome, design, giving them an old-fashioned look, solid, and comfortable. The decor and fixtures lean toward fabrics and teak rather than plastic and fiberglass. The cruisers are designed to provide extra space; for example, the big 37-ft. Prima 11/30 is built for eight, but is set up for four persons in two cabins with two toilet/showers. The other choices are the Prima 32 (sleeps four or five), and the Prima 28 for two to three persons. The large cruiser especially has a lot of class: Bow thrusters, microwave, TV/VCR, three radio/cassettes, and comes with two dinghies and bicycles.

Lochside handles its own transportation, arranged at time of booking, between Dublin or Belfast and Enniskillen, at £34 per person round trip. Also, there is bus transportation from Dublin and Belfast to Enniskillen. For boaters with cars, parking is available at the marina.

Travelers wanting to arrive a day or so before cruising can book a hotel in Enniskillen (see contact information in Towns & Highlights). Taxi fare from the town center to the boatyard is about £3.

This service is very personalized. All questions can be answered, and advice about the Loughs and rivers is knowledgeable and freely given. There is a launderette at the reception complex. In sum, we recommend this small company especially for Erne cruising, but into the Shannon–Erne Link as well. Book direct or through agents (see Appendix).

• **Carrick Craft** Other Bases: Carrick (No. Shannon), Banagher (So. Shannon), Knockninny Quay, Derrylin, Co. Fermanagh, BT92 9JU
No. Ireland
International Booking Tel: 44-28-3834-4993
Fax: 44-283-834-4995

Kinnego Marina
Oxford Island
Lurgan, BT66 6NJ
No. Ireland
E-mail: sales@carrickcraft.com
Website: www.cruise-ireland.com
Agents: UK: Blakes Holiday Boating; US: Great Trips
Unlimited, Blakes Vacations (see Appendix)
See the main profile in Chapter 5.

This is a relatively new location for Carrick Craft and the marina is new and neat. The reception area and office are in a lovely old restored manor house, standing on a gentle hillside above the jetties, overlooking a stretch of Upper Lough Erne.

A fleet of over 150 rental cruisers makes this not only the largest family-owned operation on the Shannon–Erne but also provides an extensive and good choice of rental craft.

This is a fairly good location about 11 miles from Enniskillen; what it lacks in terms of proximity to a town is made up for by being the northern boatyard of three operated by Carrick Craft. This makes it ideal for anyone wanting an itinerary that includes Lower Lough Erne, at least as far as Devenish west of Enniskillen, all of Upper Lough Erne, the Shannon–Erne Link and Lough Key, and the upper stretch of the north Shannon. Or, for that matter, it makes possible one of the longest one-way cruises on the system, from Enniskillen to Banagher.

The main cruisers among the overall fleet based in Knockninny are the Kilkenny (4+2 berth) and the Carlow (2+); these are usually the cruisers reserved for one-way north trips through the Link that can be dropped off at Carrick-on-Shannon and farther south (Banagher). For a larger cruiser, inquire well in advance.

There is a supplemental drop-off fee of IRE£45 for one-way trips. Transportation can be arranged on scheduled coaches at time of booking and is the same price between this

Knockninny Quay base and Dublin or Belfast: IRE£32 round trip, £16 one way. It is the same between their Carrick-on-Shannon base and Belfast and Dublin so it's possible to come and go in any direction, and in and out of any destination airport (except that the Shannon airport to Erne is a very long trip). Parking is available at the marina.

There are B&B's in the vicinity and accommodation can be arranged for at the time of booking for anyone who wants a night of rest before starting the cruising adventure. Or take an Enniskillen hotel (see contact information in Towns & Highlights). Taxi fare from Enniskillen is about £15.

Provisioning: Because the boatbase is not in town, a grocery order form is sent to clients by mail or fax. We suggest ordering sufficient for two or three meals, then cruising into Enniskillen at your leisure, mooring at the shopping center, and provisioning at the supermarket. There are several nice moorings for the first overnight within 30–90 minutes from the boatyard.

We recommend this as a well operated company with a fleet that includes some of the nicest cruisers in the system. For river and lake details near the other Carrick Craft boatyards, see the main profile in Chapter 5 and information about its South Shannon base in Chapter 6.

• Emerald Star–Connoisseur Cruisers

Other Bases: North Shannon, South Shannon
Belturbet, River Erne
Co. Cavan, Rep. of Ireland
Tel: 353-78-20234; Fax: 353-78-21433
E-mail: info@emerald-star.com
Website: www.emeraldstar.ie
OR www.connoisseurcruisers.co.uk
Agents: UK: Blakes Holiday Boating; US: Great Trips Unlimited, Blakes Vacations, Jody Lexow Yacht Charters, Le Boat (see Appendix)
See main profile in Chapter 5.

The northernmost base of this large company is the river marina at the foot of the central area of the river town Belturbet. Of the fleet of more than 200 cruisers belonging to this large company about a third are based here, making the selection quite complete, with a choice of ten combinations of layout and size. The cruisers are all well designed, some new, some older but well maintained. We came into Belturbet the first time from Carrick-on-Shannon, through the Ballinamore–Ballyconnell Link and into the Erne lakes on a 29-ft. Town Star class cruiser, a good starter boat for two persons on a week-long itinerary, especially through the Link. For a longer period, or for more space and comfort, we'd definitely move up to the Mountain Star, a sleek, 34-foot, wide-beam boat. For larger families or groups, the Shannon Star and the Glen Star, both the same dimension at 43-by-13.6-foot, provide the ultimate in cruising for families and traveling companions, and are excellent for the lakes. They can also be taken through the Link but cannot be taken into Lough Allen. In our view, the optimum cruiser for two couples or a family of four in terms of design and price is the Lake Star class, a 32-by-12-foot craft with separate cabins and shower/toilets, a well arranged lounge, and two helm positions. We are less attracted to the Country Star, especially for boaters with little experience.

For travelers departing on their cruise by mid-afternoon, there is a very nice overnight mooring at Crom Estate (an important stop on any itinerary). For boaters in more of a hurry, southward into the Link there is good mooring at Ballyconnell, and westward downlake are numerous choices. All are marked on the charts.

Belturbet is a busy little market town with shops, pubs, and stores, and provisioning is easy, as it's just a ten-minute walk from the marina. Groceries can be ordered in advance at the time of booking if you wish. Accommodations for a pre-departure overnight can be arranged through the company at the time of booking.

Transportation is available on scheduled coaches from Dublin and Belfast airports to the boatyard at Belturbet: IRE£30 round trip, £15 one way, children under twelve free.

For cruising one-way to the Emerald Star-Connoisseur boatyards at Carrick-on-Shannon or Portumna there is a supplemental drop-off fee of IRE£40. Start days are Wednesday, Friday, and Saturday. For other river and lake details see profiles in Chapters 5 and 6.

Book direct or through an agent (see Appendix).

• Manor House Marine & Cottages

One Base: Killadeas (N. Lower Lough Erne)
Killadeas, Co. Fermanagh
BT94 1NY, No. Ireland
Tel: 44-2868-628100; Fax: 44-2868-628000
E-mail: cruising@manormarine.com
Website: www.manormarine.com

Up the north shore of Lower Lough Erne some ten miles from Enniskillen, the elegant Manor House Hotel stands isolated on a hilltop surrounded only by meadow and forest. Formerly a nineteenth-century country manor house of great proportions, the beautifully restored building is a surprise to all who view it for the first time. At the base of the hill along the lakeshore is a marina, a reception building and, in the trees, two rows of brown brick cottages.

The cottage and cruiser rental operation is owned and very well run by Trevor Noble and his family, whose younger members, son and daughter, remain much involved in operations during the cruising season.

The location is ideal, central for exploration of the Erne lakes, from where a week can be spent cruising down-lake to Belleek and up-lake through Enniskillen, along Upper Lough Erne and the river as far as Belturbet, or into the Shannon–Erne Link. How far you travel depends of course on how much time you spend at the ancient sites on Devenish,

White Island and Inishmacsaint, walking the streets of Belleek and Enniskillen or exploring the woods of Castle Crom Estate. Good advice is available at the reception center.

The cruisers are excellent: well designed, attractively furnished and appointed, trim, neat and clean. The entire fleet is one of the best we've encountered on the waterways. There are six styles and sizes ranging from the Noble Cadet that sleeps 2+2, to the Noble Prince/Regent and Noble Captain that sleep up to eight. Like the Regent, the luxury Noble Admiral has the space for eight, but is set up to sleep six, affording extensive free space for living. For families with children, the best designs are the Captain and the President, with their wide decks and high sidewalls around open areas such as the flybridge.

Transport from and to Belfast (£32 per person round trip) and Dublin (£36) can be arranged at time of booking. There is also bus service to and from Belfast and Dublin stopping at Enniskillen; taxi to the boatyard is about £8. Groceries can be pre-ordered and will be ready on arrival; ask for a list if none comes with the booking documents. The following day moor at Enniskillen or Belleek for other grocery needs. Start days are Friday and Saturday and are the same as the pickup days at the airports and ferry terminals.

Several quiet moorings nearby are perfect for the first night out: Inishmacsaint is under an hour across the lake; a new restaurant and marina is just fifteen minutes down Rossclare Bay. Up-lake are Devenish Island for tranquility (one of our favorite spots), the Round O jetty at Enniskillen, just over an hour and a half cruising, or the jetty at the Lakeland Forum in Enniskillen (easy walk to town center, Safeway, etc.). Or—have dinner or a pub meal at the hotel on the hill and spend your first night at the marina.

Prices have dropped a bit from two years ago, ranging from £525 in low season for two persons. Typical for two couples in mid season would be the Noble Princess class at about £725.

For luxury, the Noble Admiral and Noble Captain are excellent. These are good values, and we can highly recommend Manor House Marine.

If you want a cottage stay, their cottages are like small suburban homes set along a wooded road just up from the marina, each with living room, dining room, kitchen, and entry hall in addition to the bedrooms and single bathroom. They are amply furnished and well equipped. Motor day boats are available for rent, as well as fishing gear and bicycles. Cottage rent is very modest, from about £285 per cabin per week in low season, £350 in mid, and £400 in high. Use of the 20-meter indoor pool, sauna, and other indoor facilities are booked separately.

If arriving prior to your cruise departure day, try the marvelous Manor House Country Hotel (***) that stands on the hill above the marina. Tel: 2866-621561 Fax: 2866-621545.

Ruins of Monastic community, Devenish Island, Lower Lake Erne

Or, if you prefer a pre-cruise night in Enniskillen, taxi fare from Enniskillen to the boatyard is about £10. Book direct, or in the US try Great Trips Unlimited (see Appendix).

• Erne Marine
One Base: River Erne between the Lakes
Bellanaleck Quay, Enniskillen
Co. Fermanagh
BT92 2EJ, No. Ireland
Tel: 44-2866-348267; Fax: 44-2866-348866
E-mail: info@ernemarine.com
Website: www.ernemarine.com

This is a small but old-line boat company on the Erne, having operated for over thirty years. They know the territory (and at the time we visited the manager was chairman of the Erne Charter Boat Association). The modest marina and reception center is upriver about forty cruising minutes from Enniskillen at the foot of a long road that leads from the village, a cluster of houses and a service station/grocery store.

The fleet consists of about twelve cruisers of various sizes and configurations, about half of which are newer than four years old. They are all nicely designed and well kept (two types were out when we visited and we couldn't see them, but we are confident that they would be in good shape). For two persons we recommend the Swan class and for two couples or a family of four the Ultima. The 38-ft. Royal class sleeps five in luxury, and is one of the most competitively priced large cruisers on the waterway.

The location is good and the river flows softly. For a pre-departure overnight the best choice is to stay in Enniskillen and take a taxi to the boatyard the following day (about £6).

There are numerous public moorings within 1½ hours of the boatyard, including the three in Enniskillen. Provisioning can be handled by ordering a starting supply at the time of booking, or shopping at the small grocery in Bellanaleck (a ten-minute walk), or cruising to the mooring below the shopping center in Enniskillen.

Transportation can be arranged at time of booking; £36 round trip from Dublin, £32 Belfast. Bus service is also available between those cities and Enniskillen. Book direct.

• Carrybridge Boat Company
One Base: River Erne between the lakes
Lisbellaw, Co. Fermanagh
BT94 5HX, No. Ireland
Tel: 44-2866-387034; Fax: 2866-387651

This is a small company that has committed its resources to its fleet rather than on-shore facilities, which consist of a small wooden building below a bridge that crosses one branch of the Erne, upriver about six miles from Enniskillen. The modest fleet consists of cruisers that are relatively new, of which we especially liked the 31-footer: a good interior layout, privacy, good fittings, and two helm positions. The only one we could not recommend (we tried one just like it) is the two-berth sport-type with folding canvas—nice when the sun shines, but a nuisance when it doesn't. This company, like one or two other small ones in the Erne region, can be looked to if you prefer to work personally with on-site owner/operators.

The town of Lisbellaw is too lengthy a walk with a load of groceries, so if you don't have a car, plan to cruise into Enniskillen for provisions. The Carrybridge Hotel is a small but comfortable spot across from the boatyard, Tel: 44-2866-387111. Transportation can be arranged at time of booking. Book direct.

• Aghinver Boat Company
One Base: N. Lower Lough Erne
Lisnarick, Co. Fermanagh, BT94 1JY
No. Ireland
Tel: 44-2868-631400; Fax: 44-2868-631968

We found a small marina, quite isolated, with a minimal office that was closed, so are unable to report on this company except to note that the small fleet of cruisers seemed well kept. Also, the marina is wonderfully located on a north-central bay just across from White Island (see Towns & Highlights earlier in chapter). The Drumshane Hotel (**) is nearby at Lisnarick, Tel: 44-2868-621146. Book direct.

CHAPTER 3

The Shannon–Erne Link: Crom Castle to Lough Allen

In 1994 the governments of the UK and the Republic of Ireland announced that the old 37-mile (60-km) long Ballinamore–Ballyconnell Canal connecting the majestic River Shannon in the Republic of Ireland with the exquisite chain of lakes of County Fermanagh in Northern Ireland was being reopened. For over a century the canal had been an utter ruin, choked with vegetation, the stone walls of the locks collapsed and the wooden lock gates rotted and virtually disappeared. Re-named the Shannon–Erne Link, it has greatly lengthened Ireland's grand waterway, and a new view of Ireland has become accessible to pleasure boaters.

Between 1847 and 1858 thousands of workmen with only rudimentary tools basically hand-dug the canal, designed for drainage and to open a north-south waterway linking it with other completed inland navigations. It was to be a commercial water artery for moving goods through Ireland's heartland, connecting Dublin with Belleek. Within a few years of completion the canal died, done in by technical problems and railway development.

In the late 1980s the decision was made to reconstruct the great meandering canal and £30,000,000 (US$46 million) was jointly committed by the governments of the United Kingdom, the Republic of Ireland, and the European Regional Fund.

The planners reasoned that by enhancing the countryside

Haughton's Shore, a by-way mooring on the Shannon-Erne Link

a balance could be struck between keeping the area environmentally healthy and making it accessible to the public, who could come to savor the rural countryside, lakes and wildlife from the cabins and decks of motor cruisers. To that end, enormous effort was made to tread lightly on the environment during the 1990s reconstruction; for example, much of the work with heavy machines was done from the canal channel rather than from the banks. Judging from the near-pristine beauty that we later encountered, their efforts were successful.

Speed limits and the regulated number of hire boats assure that the natural beauty of the heart of Ireland will remain undisturbed. It is obviously working as planned—there are excellent moorings, impeccable facilities, good service, and large populations of birds and other wildlife. Now the Shannon–Erne is not only the longest, but also, in our view, the most beautiful natural non-commercial waterway of Europe.

The entire area is a rich natural ecosystem of both fauna

and flora. Of its 37-mile length, only 5 miles are stillwater, eight are lakes, and the rest the quietly flowing Woodford River that empties into Upper Lough Erne in Northern Ireland.

There are sixteen new moorings, several with showers and laundry facilities for boaters. One week is normally planned for a one-way trip from the Upper Shannon and through the Erne Lakes (or vice versa), of which one and a half days is for travel along the Link itself. For a more thorough exploration of the Erne or the Upper Shannon plus a round trip through the canal, allow ten days to two weeks.

Highlights along the Way

The Ballinamore-Ballyconnell Canal and the Woodford River combine to form the Shannon–Erne Link that runs just a little shy of east–west, between the town of Leitrim in the Republic's Shannon watershed and the point in the "north" where the Woodford flows into Upper Lough Erne near Crom Castle in Northern Ireland and passes through the foothills of the low Iron Mountain range. The countryside is rural and sparsely populated, with long stretches through quiet forest, and through hilly pastureland complete with grazing sheep and cattle and an occasional farmhouse. Seven lakes lie within the route, most not much larger than a broadening of the waterway, and one, Garadice Lough, several miles long.

During the two days normally spent navigating this meandering green waterway, a jewel seems to appear around every bend: A tree-rimmed lake, swans pumping great wings as they come in low to land, a traditional farmhouse standing on a well-tended hill. Even each lock is interesting— surrounded by a picnic area, a small waterfall at the weir, a place to plant your feet on solid ground to take a stroll, or perhaps a perfect spot to tie up for the night.

Starting from Upper Lough Erne and cruising toward the southwest, the northern entry to the canal link is up the rural Woodford River. The first stop southbound is Lock No. 1

Corraquill, a tranquil introduction to the locks, from which the tree-lined river languorously winds. The first of three towns easily accessible from the waterway is **Ballyconnell** (Beal ¡tha Connell), at the foot of the Slieve Russell mountains. Having twice won the Republic's National "Tidy Town" competition says something about its nature, and a rewarding visit should include the seventeenth-century Church of Ireland. And for walkers or bikers, it's a short journey through **Killykeen Forest Park**.

Between Skelan Lock (No. 3) and Aghoo Lock (No. 4) there is an idyllic mooring at **Haughton's Shore**, a good stop for the night if the timing works out. It's a small water by-way off **Lough Garadice**, from which the view from a nearby hill captures the essence of the waterway and the countryside. Lough Garadice itself is the largest lake of the Link and one of the largest in County Leitrim. Check the navigation chart for the two islands; on the one closest to Haughton's Shore stands the ruin of **O'Rourke Castle**, on the other the ruin of a seventeenth-century church.

Ballinamore (Béal Átha Móir), in English pronounced BAL na moor, is the main town along the Link. A handsome mooring provides all amenities for boaters, and is convenient to the town and the offices of the Shannon–Erne Waterways Development (stop by—they are in a low building just above and along the quay). It's a nice town to spend time in and is ideal for a walk, provisioning, and an onshore meal in any of several good pubs and small restaurants. The **Heritage Centre** is in the County Library where they will give directions to the ruins of **Fenagh Abbey**. It is also a principal fishing center, with gear available for rent and good advice freely given.

A stop at the mooring at **Keshcarrigan** will reveal a tiny two-pub hamlet, a good restaurant, gallery and craft shop, and a good place for a walk over Sheebeg Hill and for views across the valley to Sleive an Iarainn (Iron Mountain). Ask directions from any resident to the **Letterfine House** and the **Dermot and**

Grainnes Bed, a dolmen (ancient stone monument) on the shore of Lough Scur. Along with its sister hill, Sheemore, these are the fairy hills, home to the *Sidhe*, Ireland's legendary Little People, and the subject of the hauntingly beautiful ballad "Sheemore, Sheebeg" popular throughout the country. The remains of Fionn McCumhaill (Finn McCool), a hero of folklore, reputed builder of the Giant's Causeway that once linked Ireland and Scotland, are also said to lie there. Keshkerrigan **(Lough Scur)** is at the maximum height of the Ballinamore–Ballyconnell Canal; from here the direction of the water flow changes, southwesterly into the Shannon and northeasterly into the Erne.

Just downstream of Lock No. 16 (Killarcan), tiny **Leitrim Village** lies a quarter mile from the waterway, and within five minutes cruise time beyond the bridge, the canal and the River Shannon meet. (Or, if cruising northward up the Link to the Erne, the village lies just beyond the point where the canal departs from the Shannon.)

Wildlife

Swans, kingfisher, gray herons, great crested grebes, mallards, and teal are the predominant birdlife along the canal and river portions of the waterway, the entire area being on one of the major flyways. With engines at idle as you approach the lakes, especially through the reed marshes and in the sloughs at the up-flow ends, watch for marsh hens, Canada and greylag geese, as well as the whooper swans, ducks, and other migratory birds that frequent the area.

The shallows are shown on the charts, and the reed verges are obvious. We like to nose into the reeds where there is little current, stop the engine and watch. Other marsh-dwelling birds to look for are the water rail and bittern. Where marsh edges have dried (seasonal) or drained, look for snipe and redshank. In the dryer marshes look for the lapwing, a

71

beautiful crested, black-throated, white-breasted bird that nests in spring away from the denser grass clumps. They are more common in winter in flocks, then disband in spring. Small birds include skylarks, bearded tit, reed bunting, warblers, and blackcaps. Pied wagtails can be seen bobbing in the cut grass and pebbled areas around the locks, and kestrels sweep the dryer verges and fields. One evening as we sat quietly on deck at Haughton's Shore mooring we listened to the strange cry of a cuckoo, but though we heard another when moored at Crom Castle two nights later, we failed to spot one.

Fish & Fishing

While cruising along the Link, especially the river sections and along the shores of the lakes, anglers can be seen standing in the water, or sitting on the banks or on wooden stands, fishing for the popular coarse fish: bream, roach, and rudd. Large cylindrical nets held open by rings look like misplaced windsocks, their tails in the river. These, which keep fresh the catch of the day, suggest successful fishing. Ballinamore is home to a strong angling association and is well know, among other attributes, as being the place for newcomers to start. Rental gear, bait, and advice are easy to come by. Although they are not large like the large Lough Derg and Ree, or the Erne lakes, pike can be taken in Lough Scur and Garadice. Fishing is free year around (no license required in this stretch of the waterway).

Navigation: Charts & Markers

The charts of the waterway are available in two forms: one is the Cruise Planner or Captain's Handbook, or other title given it by the boat company. It is free and is the section-by-section map of the waterway. The other form is for sale, a folding affair, essentially the same as the handbook but of larger scale. Either is fine, but look at the folding version to decide if you want to purchase it. We find them very convenient (and make a good souvenir). Both contain highly detailed, page-by-page sections of the waterway showing every rock, island, prominence, shallow, mooring, ruin, navigation marker, and lock. There is a large-scale inset for each lock and mooring, along with written comments if needed. These charts, coupled with the hundred or so carefully placed channel markers, make cruising safe and easy. The entire system is designed for ease in cruising, for the inexperienced as well as seasoned cruisers and sailors.

The navigation markers are highly visible markers installed along the Link and the waterway that tell boaters where the deep water lies; that is, they are like highway signs that signal curves, narrowing lanes or other changes in the roadway. They are placed either on buoys or at the tops of poles driven into the river or lake bottom. Not only do they serve as guides to safe water but, by displaying numbers that coincide with the charts, they help in finding your location. But this is rarely a problem in the Link, the largest expanse of water being Garadice Lough whose shores are always visible.

Note a Change in Navigation Markers: Of importance to all boaters is that the markers differ significantly in their nature between Shannon navigation and Erne navigation. The change takes place at Lough Scur in the Link, between locks 8 and 9 and is clearly marked on the charts. North of Lough Scur is Erne navigation, where the markers on each side of the waterway are large round discs painted half red, half white. The white sides of the flat plates face toward the safe water, so the key is simply to keep the boat between those white sides. In narrow water the markers come in pairs, easy to spot. In broader waters there may be a marker or series of markers on one side only, designating a shallow bay or submerged rocks; just steer to the white side. This is all made clear in the manuals and the charts.

South of Lough Scur is Shannon navigation, where the

markers are full red and full black. The reds are always on the right going downstream and the blacks are on the left. Traveling upstream, the reverse is true. The key here is simply to steer between the markers. The coloration is most helpful on the larger lakes where there is little detectable current. Although most cruisers have a compass, not all do, and the markers indicate which shoreline you are near. For example, if you are traveling upstream (red on the left) and find yourself on Lough Ree at twilight or in a morning fog, as long as the reds remain on the left (and blacks on the right), you're steering in the right direction.

The Sixteen Locks

The locks of the Link are all automatic, a blending of modern construction and modern technology. Operation is explained at the boatyard and is printed in all the Captain's Guides and cruise planners given to you at the boatyards. The first step is to *purchase at the boatyard an encrypted card for lock operation.* You will be reminded of this, but be prepared. The cost is £20 (about US$32) and each card is worth twenty units. Each lock passage takes one unit. The card also operates washing machines, dryers, and showers at certain moorings (the washer and dryer each take five units; the shower, two). This small card illustrates the modernity of the canal and of the amenities along the waterway, but also requires some basic calculations: Sixteen locks take sixteen units, leaving four units, enough for only two showers along the way. If you plan to do laundry, or prefer to use "on-land" showers rather than those on the boats, buy an extra encrypted card. *Count the units carefully,* subtracting one for each lock and any used on the wayside services, so that you won't run out before all sixteen locks have been passed through.

On arrival of your boat at the first lock at either end of the Link, it's likely that a car with the Shannon–Erne symbol on the doors will appear; a man in blue uniform will probably

A Shannon-Erne Ranger with Laura at the console for the first south lock: Killarcan

explain that although the locks are automatic, at each end of the canal a ranger will appear to explain procedures for the first time. If there is no one there, the instructions in the Captain's Handbook and on the lock operation podium are clear.

Basically, one person should be designated to pilot the boat and another to activate the locks. The duty can of course be traded off during the trip. On approaching the lock, the designated skipper pulls alongside the mooring dock and the "lockkeeper" steps off and walks up to the lock control podium that stands on the quay near the center of the lock bay. The next step depends on whether the lock gates are closed (and the red light on), or open (green light on). If open, the skipper pulls into the lock chamber, idles the engine, steps on deck and tosses the lines, first the aft then the forward, up to the lock person. The lines are looped once loosely around the on-shore post (bollard or cleat) by the lockkeeper and the ends are tossed down to the skipper (or other crew member on deck if more than two persons are on the journey). The lockkeeper then inserts the card that activates the controls and starts pushing the buttons in the sequence designated on the control panel.

The down-river gates close, water enters the walled chamber, the boat rises to the level of the up-river, the upriver gates open, the skipper (or crew-member) coils the lines in readiness for the next lock, then the skipper guides the boat out of the lock and comes alongside the up-river mooring and the designated lockkeeper jumps aboard.

If the gates are closed, the lockkeeper of the crew will have to determine if the lock is in use by another boater. Once empty, the lockkeeper must operate the controls to empty the lock and open the gate to the waiting boat. Going down-river, the sequence is reversed. This sounds a bit challenging but is good exercise and rather fun and should pose no problem for even a two-person crew whose members are able to walk up and down one or two flights of stairs.

Again, this is explained at the boatyard and in the Captain's Manual. Everything happens very slowly so there is little chance of error or damage (but the on-boat crew should keep an eye on the dinghy, avoiding the closing gates).

The locks are numbered from the northern end from one to sixteen, each also having a name: Corraquill is No. 1, Ballyconnell is No. 2, Skelan No. 3, and so forth. Killarcan No. 16 is the first lock counted from the south end of the Link.

Each lock is characterized by 40–100 yards of concrete approaches, both upstream and down, providing ample mooring. There are bollards or cleats to which boats can be tied. The chambers have stone and concrete sidewalls, great wooden gates, steps, and a rolling lawn to the control podium. Alongside each lock is the weir where water is diverted around the lock itself, usually a broad cascade with a sign posted to stay clear. The lock areas provide spots of respite from steering as well as providing the mechanisms for passage. Some have no additional amenities, but others have picnic tables, restrooms, laundry facilities, and showers. All serve as spots for overnight mooring, or just points to pull up, go ashore, picnic, explore towns, visit historic sites, or just to take a welcome walk.

A Shannon–Erne Link Itinerary

For purposes of illustration, a description of one of our first week-long itineraries will be useful. We wanted to cruise the Shannon–Erne Link and the waters that lie immediately to its south and north, so we flew into Dublin and were met by one of the Shannon–Erne minivans and taken to Carrick-on-Shannon, about a two-hour drive.

A fresh start was important to us so we planned our arrival for a day earlier than the normal Saturday turnover day and took a room at the Bush Hotel to overcome jet lag. The next morning we carried our luggage to the Emerald Star–Connoisseur boatyard, then walked back to town for groceries. At 2:00 we returned for our training and by 4:30 signed the form that said we had been checked out and knew what we needed to know. As the trainer handed us the key, we asked advice about where to moor for the night. "Go up the river for half an hour or so," he said, "and you'll see where the River Boyle comes in on your left (maybe he said "port"). Steer in there. You'll soon go through Lough Drumharlow, then continue up the Boyle under the Coothall Bridge and on up the river for half an hour to the Clarendon Lock. It's the only lock north of Carrick where you'll find a lockkeeper," he told us. "It will cost 60 pence. Be there before 8 PM (7 in the off-season) and they'll take care of you. Then after you've cleared the lock you'll be in Lough Key. After about fifteen minutes steer left and you'll see a castle on an island. You can't miss it. Across from the island you'll spot a lovely mooring at Lough Key Forest Park. Spend the night, walk through the park and the bog garden in the morning, and stop at the visitors center for coffee and a scone." That's precisely what we did. It was a splendid introduction to cruising the Upper Shannon and the Boyle.

We left Lough Key late the next morning, returned to the Shannon and turned left, or northeastward (marker to Lough Allen and Shannon–Erne). Because of a timed itinerary we passed up the round trip into Lough Allen that time, but it called for a return visit. By early afternoon we had passed the village of Leitrim and were on our way up the Link, and by 7 that evening we'd passed through locks Killarcan, Termactiernan, Dumdruff, Newbrook, Lisconor, and Kilclare where we moored for the night.

With stops at Keshkerrigan, and for lunch and groceries at Ballinamore, for our third evening (the second on the canal), we moored in a tranquil byway where a sign told us that we were at "Caladh an Hochtúnaigh" (Haughton's Shore) on the "Uisecebhealach na Sionainne-Héirne" (Shannon–Erne Waterway). It is the most attractive mooring on the Link.

By early afternoon of the following day we cruised along the Woodford River into Upper Lough Erne where we spent the night at the Crom Estate mooring. For the next three days we explored the Erne lakes, mooring at two spots at Enniskillen, going down Lower Lough Erne as far as the island of Inishmacsaint, and returned to moor again at Crom Castle before returning the cruiser at Belturbet.

This trip can of course be taken in either direction, and is best from north to south if your destination city is Belfast. Given the locks as well as the points to stop and explore, figure two days at a reasonable pace, one and a half if you don't tarry; where you tie up for the night depends on the time of day you start, but rest assured that there are moorings at all the locks as well as other spots along the route. If you want to be in a town, time yourself to moor at Ballinamore or Ballyconnell. If seeking isolation, most any other lock, plus Haughton's Shore and Aghalane Mooring (nearest Lough Erne) will do nicely.

Another good itinerary begins and ends at the town of Ballinamore in the middle of the Link, and is noted below under the Locaboat Ireland Ltd. profile.

Cruiser Line Profile

There is only one boatyard located in the Link itself, plus a narrowboat operation, both at the mid-link town of Ballinamore. The following is a new and interesting operation:

• **Locaboat Ireland, Ltd.**
The Marina
Ballinamore, Co. Leitrim
Rep. of Ireland
Tel: 011-353-78-45300; Fax: 353-78-45301
E-mail: info@locaboat.ie
Website: www.locaboat.ie
OR www.locaboat.com (Ireland & Continental)
US Agent: Le Boat (see Appendix)

Several years ago, in order to help increase the number of visitors to the pretty town of Ballinamore, especially since the opening of the Shannon–Erne Link, the community, along with the Shannon–Erne Development, built new moorings and amenities along the waterway. It then became the southern marina for servicing the cruisers of the other community owned cruiser company, Belleek Charter Cruising, and operated that way for two seasons. The next step in the development of waterway-based enterprise was the entry in 1999 of the very large French cruiser company, Locaboat Plaisance, which builds its own special kind of cruisers and has operations not only in France, but in Belgium, the Netherlands, and other European countries. Locaboat shipped a fleet of "Penichettes" from their operations in France to Ballinamore and started up their Ireland venture under an experienced Ballinamore manager and staff.

The Penichette is an interesting vessel adapted by Locaboat from the design of the Peniche, the working barges that have for centuries plied the rivers of France. On a similar hull design, what serves as cargo and living space on the Peniche has been replaced with living space for pleasure cruisers, and the overall size has of course been diminished greatly from the huge commercial haulers that gave birth to the name of their pleasure counterparts. They stand out on the Shannon–Erne Waterway because of their different shape and configuration. They are a bit boxy, but they maximize interior space, making them ideal for families and larger groups, although there are smaller ones ideal for two. They do, in fact, offer considerable versatility with six different models that sleep from two to ten persons. For non-family couples, for example, the best design for privacy is a double cabin forward and one aft. Side-deck space is a bit limited, but sun decks make outside travel and lounging on sunny days pleasurable.

Ballinamore itself is an attractive place that offers all services from restaurants and shops to renters of bicycles and advice on cruising. The mooring and marina are virtually in town, and the facilities at the mooring include showers and "launderette" operated by the encrypted card that also operates the locks. Provisioning is easy, as there are grocers in town within an easy walk of the marina (Tarpey's Central Supermarket and W.J. McWeeney will deliver to the boat).

Also at the quay is the office of Shannon–Erne Waterways Promotions, the government-created entity that does what its name says, including publishing information about the Waterway and the cruiser companies and associated support. It is open to the public.

The idea of starting a cruise at the middle of the link is a good one, making possible a choice of a week southbound into the Shannon or a week northbound into the Erne. In fact, a decision to do one or the other should be made rather than cruising north for two days, retracing the route, then south for a three-day round trip (or vice-versa). For example, a week-long round trip from Ballinamore into the Erne all the way to Belleek is feasible. Southbound, a round trip past Carrick-on-Shannon and roughly as far as Roosky and Lough Boffin is reasonable, including a side trip up the River Boyle to beautiful Lough Key, where there is good mooring. If departing from the boatyard northward at mid-afternoon we recommend Haughton's Shore for the overnight. Southbound, try Keshcarrigan or the lock at Kilclare.

Accommodation in Ballinamore makes arrival a day before starting the cruise an inviting alternative (The Commercial & Tourist Hotel is central, Tel: 353-78-44675; Fax: 78-44679, or ask the boat company to reserve for you). An alternative is to overnight at Carrick-on-Shannon (see Chapter 5, The North Shannon) and take a taxi to Ballinamore—fare about IRE£15.

Transportation arrangements can be made at the time of booking, and requires only that you provide your date, time, and location of your arrival in Dublin (or Belfast, although this is more distant). The arranged minibus service runs about IRE£20 per person, or about £120 for up to three in a taxi.

And, oh, it were a glorious thing
    To show before mankind
How every race and every creed
    Might be by love combined;
Might be combined, but not forgot
    The source from which they rose,
As filled with many a rivulet
    The Stately Shannon flows.
        —Thomas Davis (1814–1845)

CHAPTER 4

The River Shannon Overview: The Headwaters to the South End of Navigation

Beginning at least as early as the sixth century, the Shannon has been a part of the great trading route from Gaul and the middle Rhine, a waterway along whose banks the ancient communities of early Ireland grew, and whose remains can still be seen. Except for the times when storms stir the waters of the two large lakes it forms, the Shannon has become a tamed river whose principal users are the wildlife, both resident and passing, that inhabit its waters and shores and forests and the meadows it floods each year. Then there are those who live in the towns along its course, and on the farms that would not exist without the river. And there are anglers from boat and bank, and now the crews of pleasure boats who, unlike the wildfowl, not long after departing from the boatyards seem to be swallowed up by the vastness of the waterways.

Such is the length of the navigable River Shannon that for the convenience of readers and boaters this guide divides it into two chapters following this chapter's overview of its entirety.

The Countryside

The Shannon flows unrestricted from its headwaters in the Cuilcagh Mountains that lie along the north border between the Republic of Ireland and Northern Ireland. We will not enter the mild dispute on whether it flows as a trout stream from a pond in

County Cavan or from a pothole in the porous limestone across the border in County Fermanagh. It should matter not.

Even nearest its headwaters the river flows quietly, the rolling hills providing scenic beauty but no impediment to the flow. Insofar as boating is concerned, the north end of river navigation is at Battlebridge Lock, about an hour cruising time north of Carrick-on-Shannon. At that point the narrow Lough Allen Canal joins the Shannon, and is where further progress north is roughly parallel to the river via the canal and another lock leading into Lough Allen. This very large and forest-rimmed lake lies beautifully in the hills west of the lofty semi-forested Slieve Anierin, the Iron Mountain. There the deep lake, some 7-by-5-miles, deadends for boaters who must return down the canal to the Shannon system.

Four miles south of the confluence of the Lough Allen Canal with the Shannon, the volume of the river is added to by its navigable tributary, the River Boyle, that flows from Lough Key, one of the major lakes of the Shannon watershed. The Boyle and Lough Key should be on the itinerary of anyone cruising this northern stretch of the Shannon.

The lockkeeper manually powers the gate closed at Clarendon Lock between the River Boyle and Lough Key

The River Shannon Overview

From Carrick toward the south the land is rolling, often forested, with occasional riverside stretches of marshland and reeds where the stream widens into the many small lakes that characterize the river itself, the largest being Lough Boderg, Lough Bofin, and Lough Forbes. Some eight cruising hours south of Carrick-on-Shannon, near the town of Lanesborough, the waterway becomes Lough Ree, the second largest of the Shannon lakes, vast enough that caution is needed when winds have raised waves, and it is sometimes wise for cruisers to travel in pairs. A lovely island-dotted lake whose shores are unsullied, with complex lines that form bays and the inner Lakes at the southeast end, its quiet and isolated character is broken only by attractive moorings, the village of Ballykeeran and a splendid golf course near Glassan and the Killanure Point marina.

Some 16 miles south of Lanesborough, the lake become the river again, the large town of Athlone stands on both banks, and the land flattens into the Ireland midlands. The Shannon becomes slower and prone to spring flooding into the low-lying areas among the hills, providing an endless cycle of rebirth. New silt enriches the meadows, flooded areas offer nesting sanctuary to literally millions of migratory birds. As the river recedes and meadow grasses grow, the migratory birds move on, residents remain, voles and moles and rabbits move to new loose soils, followed by foxes and harriers who are at the higher end of the food chain. Along many of the hills, esker ridges can be seen, remnants of the last ice age when gravel and boulders were deposited by streams beneath the ice, after which the ice melted, leaving the deposits exposed. In this low-lying area, as deposits filled the lakes, they became shallower and smaller, many disappearing as their edges of reeds and rushes decayed into peat. On a hill just south of the town of Athlone lies Clonmacnois, site of a sixth-century monastic community and medieval university, surely one of the most serenely appealing places anywhere.

The river meanders southward through relatively flat

countryside, under the splendid sixteen-arch bridge (circa 1700), past the pretty town of Banagher, south of which it joins the Little Brosna River and forms the Shannon Callows in the vicinity of Meelick, a vast area that stretches northward and eastward to form one of the great wildlife preserves of the hemisphere, as well as an area rich in rare wild plants. There are numerous points to stop along the way. (Birders should visit the Crank House in Banagher for information on field trips.)

As the land becomes hillier and the river passes beneath the swing bridge at Portumna, again the Shannon becomes a lake—Lough Derg. A slender lake some 25 route miles long and covering 32,000 acres, it is the largest of the Shannon lakes, and a popular cruising area. Though it has a more developed shoreline than Lough Ree, it is nonetheless quite rural. With the town of Portumna at the north and the twin villages of Killaloe and Ballina at the south, plus numerous village jetties and other public moorings, Lough Derg presents an ideal expanse of water for novice boaters to begin their journey. And for anyone interested in sailing, Shannon Sailing at Dromineer on the eastern shore offers a choice of sailing yachts for rent (call Blakes at 011-44-1603-782911).

Killaloe is currently the south end of Shannon navigation for rental cruisers but a project is underway to extend downriver another 20 miles or so into the city of Limerick.

Flora

Even the stretches of the river through the flat countryside of Ireland's midlands can be fascinating to pass through, especially for anyone with an eye for the natural world. The gradation of plants from water plantain to reedmace, common reeds and into the marshy river borders that support marsh helborine, the rare blue-eyed grass, and a variety of orchids is hard to see from the land. Access usually requires slogging for considerable distances wearing rubber boots; but from the water, just nose the boat in, stop, and take in the variety. As with bird-spotting, gaining proximity to the plant and animal life of the marshes, fen, and carr is wonderfully enhanced by traveling by boat.

Some of the plants are rare, and some seem strangely out of place, such as orchids of Mediterranean origins (including some we spotted on the island of Gotland in the Baltic 1,000 miles away), and Irish fleabane, a Continental species that in Ireland is only found on the banks of Lough Derg. Other rare plants to look for are the flowering rush found around Lough Derg's Kilgarvan Quay, marsh pea (very rare except in the marshes and fenland of the central stretch of the river), and long-leaved helborine that is very rarely found elsewhere but the forests, shores, and islands of southeastern Lough Ree.

Birdlife

Birds provide common and constant companionship along the waterway, varying in their populations depending on the season. Because the entire Shannon–Erne waterway is a major stopover on the flyway, bird watchers come during spring nesting time when the waters, marshes, and fen are alive with migratory fowl. It is rare at any time to cruise for a mile without seeing the mute swans, in spring and summer with their young. In late fall and winter come Bewick's swans (especially seen along the west shore of Lough Derg), and the whoopers, a few of which stay over into the summer months (and can be distinguished by yellow on their beaks). Mergansers pass by, and migratory ducks of all stripes join the residents, along with the handsome Egyptian and barnacle geese. Along with swans, great crested grebes are among the most evident permanent residents, seen almost everywhere, along with coots, moorhens, dabchicks, herring gulls, blackbacks, black-headed gulls, and gray herons. As the marshlands dry during the early summer the kestrel and merlin appear, but perhaps the most sought-after sight is the feeding encounter of a marsh harrier pair. At nesting time from late May to mid-June the female stays with the eggs or the young while the cock is on the hunt; when he returns, rather than go to the nest he circles and calls, at which point the hen rises to meet him and they pirouette in the air as the prey is handed off.

The fens and carr that rise behind the marsh banks support literally dozens of bird species, from warblers to tits, and swifts to martins. The birds most difficult to spot are the lapwing and the rather rare corncrake, a bird much more easily heard than seen. Cormorants line rocky intrusions that reach from the shore into the lake and stand dramatically on the navigation marker posts along the river.

Harder to spot, but worth looking for are the kingfishers that breed along the smaller rivers. They become more visible throughout the water system in late summer and autumn. Pied wagtails are friendly little fellows that bob and dip in the grass and gravel areas along mooring and locks.

Various special places seem to almost singularly attract certain species: greylag geese, greenshank, and dunlin prefer the west shore of Lough Derg between Mt. Shannon and Portumna. The more rare shovelers may be spotted just south of Athlone, while the lesser black-backed gull breeds in Lough Ree.

One of the most interesting areas for birders is the Shannon Callows, which stretch northward from where the Little Brosna River enters the Shannon at Meelick Lock, just downriver of the town of Banagher. It is a vast reserve, clean and unpopulated, most easily explored by boat. Look especially for the corncrake, a bird almost extinct elsewhere that thrives in the Callows.

For more information, contact the Irish Tourist Board (Bord F·ilte) and the Northern Ireland Tourist Board in New York for information and publications on birds and birding. Also, see *The Birds of Ireland* by Gordon d'Arcy (Belfast 1986) and *An Irish Flora* by D.W.Webb (Dundalgan Press 1977).

Fish & Fishing

Serious anglers will undoubtedly want to try the Irish waters, so some brief observations are in order. There *must* be fish in the Shannon or else there would not be so many anglers, especially from the Continent, sitting on their moored cruisers in the back-bays, fishing. Nor would there be the men in rubber boots and slickers under large umbrellas sitting on small stools set in the mud among the reeds, occasionally reeling in and making an awkward cast into the nearby water. Nor large nets submerged in water and held open by rings, keeping fresh the catch of the day.

One day we saw a struggle that ended ultimately in a very large fish being brought in. We walked from our mooring to join the small crowd as the fisherman hung the struggling pike on his little scale and the indicator moved down to 23 pounds! Because it was of specimen size (over 20 pounds) he did not have to throw it back; otherwise, the limit is one fish per day and the maximum weight is 3 kilograms (6.6 pounds). We began to pay more attention.

The principal sport fish in the Shannon system are salmon and brown trout, with runs of the former taking place from March to May. Trout are fished mainly by trolling, both in the Shannon and in Lough Derg, although from mid-May to mid-June fly-fishing is at its best. Seasonal and one-day permits are available. The big river, however, is best known for pike, which are caught along the entire course but reach trophy size principally in Lough Derg. License for pike is not required but, as noted above, there is a limit. Angling for coarse fish (bream, roach, tench, perch, and rudd) is the most popular and is carried out throughout the entire system, especially the Shannon in the areas near Shannonbridge, Banagher and the stretch for several miles upriver of Portumna, as well as in Lough Derg. Large stocks of good size bream can be found in the vicinity of the Lough Derg Angling & Holiday center near Killaloe at the south end of the lake. No license is required for coarse fishing.

Tackle and bait are universally available for rent from either the boat company or a nearby supplier. An angling guide and map and more detail can be obtained through the Irish Tourist Board in New York or by contacting Shannon–Erne Waterway Promotions at 011-353-61-361555.

Navigation

The 170-mile (275-km) navigable portion of the Shannon includes eighteen lakes and drops only 490 feet (150 m) from its headwaters to sea level. Along the entire route from the start of the Lough Allen canal in the north to Killaloe in the south are only five locks, all operated by lockkeepers, easy to pass into and through. There is one keeper-operated lock on the River Boyle, and three on the narrow Lough Allen canal.

Each cruiser company gives the boaters a Captain's Handbook or Manual that contains details on every aspect of operation and navigation on the waterway. Included are pages of navigation charts that delineate every boatyard, marina, mooring, island, dangerous rock, jetty, shallow bay, town location, historic site, fuel and watering point, and navigation marker, plus pubs, restaurants, overhead wires, reeds, and woods. Each marina and lock, and any other point that need special attention, is expanded and shown in even greater detail. As good as these charts are, we suggest purchasing the folded *Navigational Guide to the Shannon* for the section or sections of the river you will be cruising. Prepared by ERA-Maptec Ltd, of Dublin, and put out by IBRA, the Irish Boat Rental Association, they are easier to manage than the Manual and a handsome memento to keep after your return home.

Although much information will be provided at the time of checking out the boat, the most important tips we can offer, especially to newcomers to motor cruising the Shannon, are:

• Navigation Markers: (1) Remember that when moving *upstream* and *into* bays and harbors, the RED Markers are on the LEFT. (2) When moving *downstream* and *out of* bays and harbors, the RED Markers are on the RIGHT. The Black markers will of course be located opposite, but it's easier to remember, especially in event of emergency, that upstream red is left and downstream red is right. (These rules change northward from the Ballinamore–Ballyconnell Canal (as explained in Chapter 3).

• When mooring in a stream, always come into the bank (quay, dock, wharf) with the bow upstream. If you are traveling downstream, this will of course require passing the mooring point and making a near 360 degree turn. When you match the speed of the current, your cruiser is stopped in the water and very little of a violent nature will happen at zero speed.

• When entering a lock or approaching a mooring, for that matter, slow down but do not cut forward power. Without some forward throttle the steering is lost. If traveling too fast, use reverse to slow, but then return to forward to continue moving water past your rudder.

• When mooring alongside a jetty slip, touch the bow to the jetty, turn the wheel opposite to the slip you want to tie alongside of, and apply a bit of forward throttle. Without tying up, the boat will sit there for hours until it runs out of fuel. There's plenty of time to step ashore and secure the lines.

• Don't be afraid to tie up to some appealing bank that has no formal constructed mooring—use the stakes or anchor that comes with the boat, or tie to a tree or post. Study the chart and watch for shallow water. Swans feed in water no deeper than their necks are long, so avoid going into waters where swans are feeding.

Locks & Movable Bridges

Along the main stem of the Shannon the locks are far enough apart that with a little planning their hours of operation should not impede keeping to an itinerary. Nevertheless, the hours must be heeded. The exact dates noted below may vary slightly from year to year, so be sure to obtain the latest information at any marina.

Dates	*Monday–Saturday*	*Sunday*
Mar 14 to Apr 3	9 AM–6:30 PM	10:30 AM–4 PM
Apr 4 to Sept 25	9 AM–8:30 PM	9 AM–6 PM
Sept 26 to Nov 1	9 AM–7:30 PM	10 AM–4 PM
Nov 2 to Mar 13	9 AM–12:30 PM	10AM–12:30 PM

The only variance in the Shannon system is the Portumna Swing Bridge at the north end of Lough Derg that opens at specific times to let river traffic through. It is open for roughly fifteen minutes depending on river traffic:

Dates	*Monday–Saturday*	*Sunday*
Mar 14 to Apr 3	9:45 & 11 AM; 12:30, 2:30, 4:30 & 5:30 PM	11 AM; 12:30, 2:30 & 4:30 PM
Apr 4 to Sept 25	9:45 & 11 AM; 12:30, 3, 5:30 & 7:30 PM	11 AM; 12:30, 3 & 4:30 PM
Sept 26 to Nov 1	9:45 & 11 AM; 12:30, 3, 5 & 6:30 PM	11 AM: 12:30, 2:30 & 4 PM
Nov 2 to Mar 13	9:45 & 11 AM; 12 PM	11 AM; 12 PM

If you miss an opening of the bridge, there are moorings on both sides, so just tie up, take a stroll, talk with fellow boaters, and enjoy the respite while waiting.

Cruising Times

Assuming no stops and maximum cruising speed, the approximate one-way cruise times in hours between key points on the Shannon south of the Link, downriver to the present end of hire-cruiser navigation at Killaloe are shown below.

Realistically, with the towns to stop by and explore, a half day for monastic Clonmacnois, inlets and estuaries leading off the great Shannon lakes, the inner lakes of lower Lough Ree, the forest walks to take, Lough Key, the pubs and restaurants to enjoy, the pauses for photography, the picnics, the best way to figure travel time is to assume an average of about 5 hours cruising per day. For example, although it's possible to travel from Killaloe up Lough Derg to Portumna and back in 14 hours of non-stop cruising, a three-day minimum should be figured for the trip, giving time to visit the little towns of the lakeshore. For other illustrations, refer to the sample itineraries in Chapter 1.

If planning a single starting and ending boatyard, we recommend making the best time going and a slower return, noting places and sites outbound that you want to return to. In this way of pacing yourself there will be no need to worry about missing a particular site because of a final rush to return the boat. A good plan is to spend the last night moored within a few hours of your home base.

The following are average non-stop cruising times between the stretches north to south; for a total time between extremes, add the legs, e.g., between Leitrim and Lanesborough add 1 + 4 + 4 = 9 cruising hours (see Appendix for Average Cruising Times for the entire waterway system.)

Lough Allen Round	1 day
River Boyle/Lough Key Round Trip	1 day
Leitrim to Carrick-on-Shannon	1 hour
Carrick-on-Shannon to Roosky	4 hours
Roosky to Lanesborough	4 hours
Lanesborough to Hodson Bay	3 hours

Hodson Bay to Athlone	½ hour
Athlone to Clonmacnois	2 hours
Clonmacnois to Banagher	3 hours
Banagher to Portumna	3 hours
Portumna to Mountshannon	5 hours
Mountshannon to Killaloe	2 hours

Two cruiser companies also have boatyards in the Erne waterway system north of the Shannon–Erne Link; approximate non-stop one-way cruising times are:

Portumna to Belturbet (Erne)	35 hours (Emerald Star–Connoisseur bases)
Banagher to Knockkninny (Erne)	39 hours (Carrick Craft bases)

Cruiser Companies

In the next two chapters on the North and South Shannon, the boat companies are listed in order of their main boatyard locations along the waterway, from north to south.

The weir at Clarendon, the only lock on the River Boyle

CHAPTER 5

The North Shannon: Leitrim & Lough Allen South to Athlone

A quarter mile downstream of the **Leitrim Bridge** is the confluence of the River Shannon and the Ballinamore–Ballyconnell Canal, now called the Shannon–Erne Link. This is the southern entry point to the Link that connects the Shannon with the Erne River and lakes of Northern Ireland. The Shannon is fairly narrow at this point and runs almost due north to its headwaters in the mountains, and southward toward Carrick-on-Shannon and beyond, while the canal takes off to run almost east-west. The right arm of the "Y" on charts and maps is the Link—the left arm is the river that again separates a half mile upstream where the narrow **Lough Allen Canal** begins at the Battlebridge lock. Direction signs to the entry of the short canal are easy for boaters to spot from the river, and it is all well charted. Lough Allen is the northernmost lake of the Shannon system, a large expanse of water recently made accessible to hire cruisers by the installation of another state-of-the-art lock in the canal near the village of Drumshanbo. In one sense, the lake is separate from the flow of the two strands of the waterway (the Shannon and the "Link"), in that it requires a side trip to visit it. The surroundings are beautifully rural, forested and hilly, with relatively little development in terms of moorings, picnic sites and the like, although there is a pontoon mooring and the **Lough Allen**

Outdoor Pursuits Centre for windsurfing and water skiing. More mooring points will surely be established as the area develops, but at this time the main draw is for anglers. The very pretty village of **Drumshanbo**, a short walk from the lock and the mooring at Acres Lake, is itself a major fishing center as well as being well worth a visit for its shops, pubs, and the visitor center.

Important Note: the canal leading to Lough Allen is too narrow to handle some of the cruisers, so be sure to check with the boatyard. At this stage, we suggest that a round trip to the lake be taken only if you have plenty of time to otherwise cover your itinerary. It is a dead end and even a short trip will take 4 to 5 hours.

The **River Boyle** flows from the west into the Shannon between the Lough Allen canal and the town of **Carrick-on-Shannon** (less than an hour cruising from Carrick). It is a graceful stream, easy to navigate, much of it through wooded land, some of it forming the good-sized **Lough Drumharlow** and smaller **Oakport Lough**. Up the Boyle about half an hour is **Coothall**, where there is a public mooring and a private one

Cruisers moored at the harbor at Dromod village on Lough Bofin, North Shannon

at a pleasant waterside restaurant (overnight permitted at the former, permitted at the latter if you stop for a bite at the restaurant). Between the Coothall and Knockvicar bridges (about 2 miles apart) is the Shannon–Erne Waterway Holidays marina (see profile, below). Next up the river is **Clarendon Lock**, a handsome work completed in 1847 and operated by a lock keeper for a fee of 60 pence (US$1, hours 9 AM–8 PM April through Sept. 25; to 7:30 PM other months— check with the boatyard). There is good mooring above and below the lock, from which a path and small road leads to a general store at **Knockvicar** village (five minutes).

The lock water level at full is the level of **Lough Key**, a gem of a lake in forested country that is one of the most appealing of the waterways system. It is an excellent first night mooring out of Carrick-on-Shannon, or from the Shannon Erne Waterway Holidays marina noted above, half an hour down the Boyle, or from the Tara Cruisers marina in an inlet off the north shore just ten minutes from Clarendon Lock. The best and most scenic moorings are at the south shore, two on the mainland at **Lough Key Forest Park** and one just across the bay from these at Drumman's Island. In strong northerly winds, moor at the latter. There is a visitor's center at the south mooring, and the park itself offers a wealth of natural, historic and archaeological high points, detailed at the visitor's center. It is well worth a slow walk through. As for the origin of the Boyle, we like the version that Lough "Key," from which it flows, derives from Cé, Druid of Nuadha of the Silver Arm, who legend says drowned when the lake erupted from the earth. Actually, the Boyle continues westward toward its headwaters, and at the time of this writing is being deepened into the town of **Boyle** and should be completed by now. A visit to Boyle is important and must include a visit to **King House**, a beautifully restored early eighteenth-century manor.

If not cruising with the Lough Key based Tara Cruisers, a round trip journey from the Shannon along the River Boyle and into Lough Key should definitely be included in North Shannon itineraries.

Carrick-on-Shannon is an interesting old town, bustling and full of small shops, grocers, and cafes. On the outskirts, however, development is occurring fairly rapidly. As with the whole of County Leitrim, the town has been relatively poor, but with its river, bridge and newfound vigor as a boating center it provides a pleasant stop, full of stores and shops (many of them reminiscent of American small-town department stores of several decades past). St. George's Church dates from 1698, and at the corner of Bridge and Main street is one of the world's smallest chapels. Across the river are the ruins of fifteenth-century Creevelea Abbey. With the reopening of the Ballinamore–Ballyconnell Canal (the Link), just one cruising hour north, Carrick has become the principal hire-boat headquarters of the Shannon, an ideal starting point for cruising, especially northbound into the Link and on to the Erne, but southbound as well, especially for anglers. The proximity of the town center to the boatyards makes provisioning easy. The boatyards of Emerald Star–Connoisseur, Carrick Craft, and Crown Blue Line stretch along the riverbank. Consider arriving in Carrick for an overnight before departing for the cruise. The **Bush Hotel** is downtown; Tel: 353-78-20014; Fax: 78-21180.

Downriver, ten minutes from the entry to the short Jamestown Canal, historic **Jamestown** is worth a stop on a pleasant day. Navigation ends at the bridge and the mooring spot is fairly narrow, but it's a just a short walk into town. Three hours downriver of Carrick, ideal for a first night out for southbound cruisers, is a good harbor and mooring at **Dromod**, a tidy village that has done an excellent job of helping to make the riverside attractive. A five-minute walk from the marina is an excellent restaurant, a pub, and some small food stores. Beginners should moor in the larger harbor to the left of the entry. The other is also good, but a bit tight to turn in if the wind is blowing.

Leading from the west of Lough Boderg are two inlets, one leading to Kilglass and the other to Grange, and both are dead-ends. Whether or not to cruise up either depends on your interest in exploring, the time you have, and the weather, but they both make for pleasant journeys, especially when the sun is shining.

South of Dromod are the villages of **Roosky** and **Tarmonberry**, both attractive small places. Whether or not to venture in and tie up depends on your inclinations and the weather, or the need for a break, for a pub, or to resupply groceries or fishing supplies. There are mooring quays both up- and down-river of the Tarmonberry lock and bridge.

The next town south is **Lanesborough**, its power plant stack visible for miles. While this is an eyesore, anglers like the swarms of fish that abound in the warm water discharge. There is a small harbor and floating cafe, but unless you are an angler there is little need to spend time there.

Passing under a lift bridge along the west bank of the Shannon at Lanesborough

Lough Ree is some eight cruising hours south of Carrick-on-Shannon. Sixteen miles long, this second largest of the Shannon *loughs* makes for fine cruising, but is also large enough that care is needed if winds are strong. The countryside is very rural, and there are many bays and inlets to explore, yet a scarcity of mooring spots makes some planning necessary for deciding where to spend a night. That is, avoid departing northbound from Athlone or Hodson Bay, or southbound from Tarmonberry or Lanesborough unless there is three hours of light left in the evening. It's risky to be caught on the lake by darkness.

At the southwest end of Lough Ree is a mooring at **Hodson Bay**, an excellent stop if only to go into the immense four-star **Hotel Hodson Bay** for lunch, a pub supper, or elegant dinner. It's a surprise to see such a large and attractive hotel standing alone a hundred yards from the small marina. For overnight in the marina, plan to arrive early as it's very popular. And if northbound be aware that this is the last cozy mooring before a 2 ½-hour long stretch along the length of Lough Ree, to the mooring at Lanesborough.

To the east across Lough Ree are the **Inner Lakes**, whose quiet and isolated character is broken only by a few moorings. One is at the harbor of the village of **Ballykeeran** where groceries, pubs, and services can be found. Another mooring is near the seventeenth hole of the splendid golf course of the **Glasson Country Club**, where the restaurant, as well as the golf course, is available to boaters. At Killinure Point at the entry to the inner lakes is the marina for Waveline Cruisers and at Mucknagh Point is the Lough Ree Cruisers boatyard. Both are profiled in the following section.

Athlone, the next town downriver is the largest on the Shannon and is very worth a stopover, even if only for an hour or two, but longer if possible to give the place its due. It stands astride the river just below where Lough Ree becomes the Shannon again. At the north outskirts is the Jolly Mariner

Marina, boatyard of Athlone Cruisers and quayside restaurant. Athlone was founded during the early thirteenth century, but much of the remaining wall dates from the early seventeenth century, and remnants can be seen along Northgate and Dublingate streets. There are good moorings on both sides of the river near the town center, both above and below the Athlone lock. To most easily tour the town sites, stop by the Information Center just up from the west bank mooring. If no space is available, tie up at the east bank and walk across the bridge. Most important to visit are thirteenth-century **King John's Castle and Museum** and the three old churches. Directions are in the walking guide available at the Information Center. There are many shops, stores, and services in this interesting old town. Athlone is the birthplace of the famed singer John McCormick.

If planning to arrive a day or so prior to your cruising date out of the Athlone area boatyards, following are a few good hotel choices in the vicinity (phone/fax from the US & Canada dial 011-353-):

Ballykeeran Lakeside Hotel, Ballykeeran, near Athlone
Tel: 902-85163
Hodson Bay Hotel, near Athlone
Tel: 902-92444; Fax: 92688
E-mail: info@hodsonbayhotel.com
Website: www.hodsonbayhotel.com
Prince of Wales Hotel, Church Street, Athlone
Tel: 902-72626; Fax: 75658
Royal Hotel, Mardyke Street, Athlone
Tel: 902-72924; Fax: 75194

Cruising Times

The following times are for non-stop cruising at an average speed of 5 mph. For a table of times between key points of the full length of the Shannon, as well as sample itineraries, see Chapter 4, in the section on cruising times. The following are for the North Shannon region that lies between Leitrim and Athlone. Lough Allen and Lough Key are side trips off the Shannon. (See Appendix for Average Cruising Times for the entire waterway system.)

Lough Allen Round	1 day
River Boyle/Lough Key Round Trip	1 day
Leitrim to Carrick-on-Shannon	1 hour
Carrick-on-Shannon to Roosky	4 hours
Roosky to Lanesborough	4 hours
Lanesborough to Hodson Bay	3 hours
Hodson Bay to Athlone	½ hour

Getting to the Boatyards

Transportation from and to Belfast and Dublin can be arranged through all the hire boat companies. This is usually by means of a van, minibus, or coach that collects clients at the terminals of the principal airports and ferryports. All flight arrival information must be given to the boat company, which, in turn, schedules the pickups at the appropriate arrival lounge or baggage area. If planning to spend time in Dublin or Belfast prior to departing for the boatyard, discuss with the cruiser agent the place to meet the minibus. Cost of one-way transportation runs about IRE£15 to IRE£20 per person, double that for round trip (called "return" by the British and Irish). This is the typical and best way of transport for travelers without a vehicle. Unless otherwise noted in the profiles, this means of transfer is available from the cruiser company.

All the boatyards at Carrick-on-Shannon and the two

near Knockvicar/Coothall (Tara and Shannon–Erne Waterway Holidays) are best served in and out of Dublin, but the distance to Belfast is not much farther. It's possible to arrange any itinerary at the time of booking, that is, in and out of Dublin or Belfast, or in one and out the other.

The boat base at Athlone (Athlone Cruisers) is so far from Belfast that arranging transport doesn't make sense; Dublin is close, and even passing through Shannon airport is feasible.

Be alert to the cruising start days of the company you book with, and even to the start days of particular cruisers. Saturdays are the norm, but more and more companies are adding other days of the week, most often giving a choice between Wednesday, Friday, and Saturday.

When flexible trip scheduling is possible, the approach we recommend is to plan to arrive in your airport destination city a day or two in advance of the cruising start day. Arrange in advance with the boat company your transportation for that day, then book a hotel in Carrick-on-Shannon, Athlone, or a B&B near the boatyard for a night to orient yourselves and get over jet lag, and go to the boatyard the following day. If a hotel contact for your destination is not shown in this guide, boat companies will usually either book a room for you, or will recommend an accommodation.

There is also rail service between Dublin (Connolly Station) and Carrick-on-Shannon, and between Dublin (Heuston) and Athlone, as well as Bus Éirean out of Dublin's Busaras Station. We suggest, though, using the boat company transfer if you are departing for the boatyard immediately upon arrival—arranging rail or bus after all night on the jet isn't worth the few Irish punts you might save.

For visitors who choose to rent a car, no boatyards along the Shannon system are so distant from Dublin that driving to them is too inconvenient. It's about 100 miles (163 km) between Dublin and Carrick and 80 miles (130 km) between Dublin and Athlone.

Ideal First Night Moorings from Carrick-on-Shannon

Three cruiser companies are based at Carrick-on-Shannon: Carrick Craft, Emerald Star–Connoisseur, and Crown Blue Line. Typical first-day departure time is mid-afternoon, which suggests seeking a good overnight mooring spot within two or so hours of the marina, depending on the season. Twilight can linger as late as 9 PM during the summer months.

Downriver, the closest mooring is at Jamestown, but the river is narrow and the small marina is often crowded. An alternative for a close spot is down the Jamestown Canal to the Albert Lock where there are mooring docks both above and below the lock. Just beyond (30 minutes cruising) is a small mooring at Carnadoe Quay, but if time permits, make a run to the very nice Dromod Harbor (3 hours from Carrick). If possible, tie up at the larger of the two harbors that lie within the single entry.

Castle Island, near the mooring at Lough Key Forest Park

Upriver, we recommend steering into the River Boyle, which joins the Shannon from the west some 30 minutes north of Carrick, and mooring at Coothall, or just below Clarendon Lock. Or ideally, if time permits, into Lough Key then south toward Castle Island to Rockingham Forest Park (also called Lough Key Forest Park) where there are three good moorings, two along the shore and one on Drumman's Island. As from the two preceding marinas at Coothall and in

Lough Key, boaters who want to bypass the Boyle and Lough Key and proceed upriver, the two best moorings are at Battlebridge for travelers into Lough Allen, and at Leitrim for travelers eager to start through the Shannon–Erne Link.

CRUISER LINE PROFILES

The cruiser companies of the Shannon offer a very wide variety of boats to choose from, some of which are new, some older, but all that we cruised in, inspected in boatyards and looked at in moorings along the way, appeared to be well kept. Most of the companies are small to middle size and family owned and operated (Athlone Cruisers, Silver Line, Waveline, Shannon–Erne Waterway Holidays, and Tara Cruisers). One is large and family owned (Carrick Craft), and the other two are either large companies or owned by large companies (Emerald Star–Connoisseur Cruisers, Crown Blue Line). Insofar as service is concerned, ownership appears to make little or no difference; the reception areas at the boatyards may be more elaborate for the larger companies, and certainly the fleets of Carrick Craft and Emerald Star–Connoisseur Cruisers are larger. But we found no boat companies on the Shannon that we would not be pleased to book with, nor any without an adequate selection of cruisers. Thus, your choice is an individual one, based principally on where you want to cruise, convenience of the boatyard to your destination airport or ferryport in Ireland, personal taste in cruiser style and appearance, and budget.

As for choosing one particular region or stretch of waterway, after reading the Highlights sections (and other general guides to Ireland) decide which is of most interest to you. If, for example, you are especially interested in birdlife and nature preserves and cruising the large lakes, trophy fishing and the monastic ruins at Clonmacnois, starting out of Athlone or one of the two marinas of the Inner Lakes near Ballykeeran is a good idea. If a trip through the Link and a taste of the Erne lakes is important, then one of the companies at Carrick-on-Shannon, Lough Key, or Knockvicar is the best choice. Beyond that, look at cruiser configurations and prices in the brochures and websites, as well as selection. Value is important: Crown Blue Line cruisers, for example, are among the most expensive (comparing boats of similar size and berths), but are among the most deluxe. Watch also for the different seasonal prices. They vary from year to year, but it's possible for a company to have the cheapest low-season rates and yet have among the highest prices at peak season. The choice is not unlike renting a car: Large, small, standard, or deluxe.

Security deposits are required by all the hire boat companies, ranging between £150 and £350 depending on the size of the vessel. This refundable deposit can be made by credit card—the charge simply not recorded unless the boat is returned damaged. An option is to purchase damage insurance.

The following boat rental companies are listed from north to south. Except as noted with a +44 (UK country code), all telephone and fax numbers are preceded by the international access code plus the Republic of Ireland country code 353; e.g., from the US and Canada, for Tara Cruisers dial 011-353-78-21369; for Carrick Craft international booking office in Northern Ireland, dial 011-44-28-3834-4993.

- **Tara Cruisers**
One Base: North Shannon/River Boyle
The Moorings, Lough Key
Knockvicar, Carrick-on-Shannon
Co. Leitrim, Ireland
Tel: 353-78-21369; Fax: 353-78-21284
E-mail: tarac@iol.ie www.ibi.ie/tara

Set in one of the most beautiful areas of the entire Shannon–Erne Waterway system, Tara Cruisers is a comparatively small company operating about twenty-one cruisers from the single base on the north shore of Lough Key, just northwest of Carrick-on-Shannon. The marina is five minutes cruising time above the Clarendon Lock, which lifts and lowers boats between the River Boyle and Lough Key. It has been in operation for six years, but recently moved its headquarters to its present location.

The office and the attractive atrium reception room are a one-minute walk from the harbor, sharing the location with a very nice restaurant and pub called The Moorings, owned and operated by the company.

There are only two classes of cruisers available at present, both large, spacious, weighty, and steel-hulled. The Tara 36 has four berths in two cabins, plus one convertible berth in the lounge, and the Tara 42 sleeps six in three cabins plus one convertible. Both have 80-hp diesels, dual hydraulic steering positions, and central heat. They are well laid out and nicely fitted, although a few of the older ones are beginning to show a little superficial wear, so you may want to ask for their newest available. These big craft offer unusually comfortable cruising, and the price is very good for the size and quality. They come with a dinghy but outboards are extra with the 36-footer; TV, fishing gear, cell phones, and bicycles can be rented.

Provisioning: Because the boatbase is not in town, a grocery order form is sent to clients by mail or fax. We suggest it be filled and returned, ordering sufficient for two or three meals. However, there is a small general store in Knockvicar, a fifteen minute walk, where enough food for a couple of days can be found, certainly enough to last until you cruise into Carrick-on-Shannon, or north into Ballinamore, to moor and buy groceries.

Transportation can be arranged at the time of booking for any combination of arrivals and departures from, or to Dublin and Belfast, ranging in cost from about IRE£15 to £18 per person each way. Vehicles can be parked for the cruise duration, or Hertz and Avis will deliver a rental car to the marina for about £45 to mesh with the end of cruising.

Start day is normally Saturday with pickup about 4 PM, but special arrangements can be made for overseas clients.

The big cruisers may be a bit intimidating for first-time boaters, but this can be overcome with a little practice on Lough Key before departing into the Shannon. The largest cruiser cannot be taken into Lough Allen.

Assuming a mid-afternoon departure on the first cruising day, the nearest best moorings for the night are across Rockingham Forest Park (also called Lough Key Forest Park) where we recommend any of three good moorings, one on Drumman's Island. Downriver it's easy to make Coothall. Figure 2 hours cruising to Carrick-on-Shannon if you want to skip Lough Key.

We recommend this company—it's an easy operation and the owner/operators, Des Gillette and Harriet Sims, and the crew are very helpful.

• Shannon Erne Waterway Holidays Ltd.

Bases: North Shannon & Lower Lough Erne
Knockvicar (Coothall), River Boyle
Co. Roscommon, Ireland
Tel: 353-79-67028; Fax: 353-79-67333
E-mail: sewh@eircom.net
Website: www.sew-holidays.com
No. Ireland Base:
Tel: 44-2868-641507; Fax: 44-2868-641734
E-mail: helen@boatingireland.com
Website: www.irelandboating.com

This boatyard is near the village of Knockvicar, about 10 road miles (1½ hours by cruiser) from Carrick-on-Shannon. The marina lies between two bridges, Coothall Bridge and Knockvicar Bridge, which span the River Boyle upstream some dozen miles from its confluence with the Shannon.

The North Shannon

The little towns of Coothall and Knockvicar, as well as the Clarendon Lock and Lough Key, are within a ten-minute walk along wooded paths and a small paved road.

The association of two companies, this one in the Republic south of the Link and Erincurrach Cruising on Lower Lough Erne, gives boaters the option of one-way cruising between two choice locations, making it especially ideal for a week. Some of the cruisers are owned independently by the company, and another eleven or so are jointly owned with Erincurrach, the combination resulting in a good selection for round trip cruising. Only the Devenish class (2+2 berths) and Tully class (6+2 berths) are available, though, for the one-way itineraries. We see this as no problem, as both cruisers are excellent and the prices are fair. Departure from either marina is fine, with this one more convenient for arrivals at Dublin airport, and the Erne base for Belfast arrivals.

This is a small family operation, run in a style that assures personal attention in terms of getting to know the waterways, advice on moorings, places to visit and, of course, getting the right cruiser and how to handle it.

Transportation can be arranged for any combination of arrivals and departures from and to Shannon, Dublin, and Belfast, ranging in cost from about IRE£30 to £35 per person round trip. Vehicles can be parked, or will be transported between the marinas for one-way cruisers.

Friday and Saturday start days are offered, and transport from and to Belfast can be arranged at time of booking. Pick up days are Wed., Fri., and Sat. There are also three to five departures daily by rail and by Bus Éirean between Dublin and Carrick-on-Shannon, about 12 road miles from Knockvicar.

Nearby accommodation can be arranged for at the time of booking for anyone who wants a restful night before departing by boat. The company will transport clients. Or stay in Carrick (Bush Hotel Tel: 78-20014; Fax: 78-21180). Given the tranquility of the area, though, it is not difficult to arrive, take the training, and travel half an hour to the Lough Key Forest Park mooring for the night.

Provisioning: Because the boatbase is not in town, a grocery order form is sent to clients by mail or fax; we suggest ordering sufficient for two or three meals. There is a small general store just ten minutes walk in Knockvicar, or cruise into Carrick-on-Shannon at your leisure to moor and buy groceries.

We recommend this as an attractive and well-maintained fleet—we like all the cruisers and especially the area. Owners/Managers are Paddy and Maria Gilboy. Book with this office or, if planning a one-way cruise, either here or with its partner Erincurrach Cruisers at Lough Erne: Tel: 44-2868-641737; Fax: 44-2868-641734.

A start from this marina, whether one-way or round trip, should definitely begin in the upriver direction prior to going into the River Shannon. Cruise up through the Clarendon Lock and into Lough Key, one of the most beautiful lakes of the waterway system (see Lough Key in the Highlights section, above). After exploration, or an overnight mooring, return down the Boyle to the Shannon.

The best moorings for the first overnight are up the River Boyle, through the lock, and after ten minutes steer south across Lough Key toward the visible Castle Island to Rockingham Forest Park (also called Lough Key Forest Park) where there are three good moorings, plus one on Drumman's Island. Downriver, the Boyle meets the Shannon. Up-Shannon, the two best moorings are at Battlebridge for travelers into Lough Allen and at Leitrim for travelers planning to go through the Shannon–Erne Link. They are equidistant, less than an hour from Coothall. Down-Shannon, the first moorings are at Carrick-on-Shannon. As a courtesy to all boaters, it is permissible to moor at boatyards of other cruiser companies, but tie up at the most distant jetty from the center of their operations.

For river and lake details near the Erne base see the Erincurrach Cruising profile in Chapter 2.

• Carrick Craft

Bases: North Shannon, South Shannon, Upper Lough Erne
The Marina
Carrick-on-Shannon
Co. Leitrim, Rep. of Ireland
International Booking (No. Ireland):
Tel: 011-44-283-834-4993; Fax: 44-283-834-4995
Main Office: Kinnego Marina, Oxford Island
Lurgan, BT66 6NJ
No. Ireland
E-mail: sales@carrickcraft.com
Website: www.cruise-ireland.com
Agents: UK: Blakes; US: Blakes Vacations, Great Trips Unlimited (see Appendix)

The headquarters and reception area is 100 yards from the marina that occupies a lengthy stretch of the riverbank less than a five-minute walk from the center of town. In town are several convenient grocery stores, all an easy walk to the marina, so provisioning is easy. Try the delicious Irish soda bread.

This is a large and busy marina but easy to deal with, consisting of a number of jetties just below the reception office. The service is good and the staff helpful, so if on returning your cruiser there appears to be no space, just idle in and float—someone will spot you and lend a hand with mooring.

A fleet of over 150 rental cruisers makes this not only the largest family-owned operation on the Shannon–Erne, but also provides a wonderful choice of rental craft.

As at the other two Carrick Craft boatyards, the service here is very good. We found the staff helpful and informative, the instructors friendly and professional, and the cruisers well maintained. At the southern base at Banagher, the marina is shared with Silver Line Cruisers.

There are at present nine classes of cruisers to choose from, ranging from the very small, economy Dublin class to the large (eight berth) elegant Clare class. Unless you are on a very tight budget and plan to travel light, we can't recommend the little 24-ft. Dublin. Instead, for two persons we suggest a small step up to the 27-ft. Carlow class, which has a better overall design as well as more interior space. For three to four persons on a budget the Kerry class is fine except that it has a single aft steering position open to the elements unless the fabric hood is erected.

We took a 34-ft. Kilkenny class from Banagher up to Carrick and found it to be a delight, so much so that we will take one up the link next year. Easy to steer, dual helm and modern design. It is luxury for one couple and perfect for two couples or a family of four or five needing two private cabins, each with shower and WC. Their newest cruiser is the deluxe Waterford, a 6+2 berth beauty that makes boating a true pleasure.

The Kilkenny (4+2 berth) and the Carlow (2+) are usually the cruisers reserved for one-way north trips through the Link for drop-off at the Erne base at Knockninny. There is a supplemental drop-off fee of IRE£40.

Transportation can be arranged on scheduled waterway coaches (bus or minibus) at time of booking and is the same price between Carrick-on-Shannon and either Dublin or Belfast: About IRE£32 round trip, £16 one way. It is the same between their Erne base and Belfast and Dublin so it's possible to come and in go in any direction and in and out of any destination airport. The Banagher base can be served out of Shannon International Airport as well as Dublin. Shannon is far too distant to serve Erne boatyards.

Provisioning is easy at any of several stores in Carrick-on-Shannon. Security deposits may be paid by credit card and range between IRE£200 and £400. Damage insurance can be purchased instead.

For river and lake details for this and other boatyards at

Carrick-on-Shannon, see the preceding section, Ideal First Night Moorings from Carrick-on-Shannon.

For river and lake details near the other Carrick Craft boatyards, see the company listings in Chapters 2 & 6.

• Emerald Star–Connoisseur Cruisers
Bases: North & South Shannon, River Erne
The Marina
Carrick-on-Shannon
Co. Leitrim, Rep. of Ireland
Tel: 353-78-20234; Fax: 78-21433
E-mail: info@emerald-star.com
Website: www.emeraldstar.ie
OR www.connoisseurcruisers.co.uk
Agents: UK: Blakes; US: Great Trips Unlimited, Blakes Vacations, Jody Lexow Yacht Charters, Le Boat (see Appendix)

The main base and headquarters of this large company at Carrick-on-Shannon is geographically above the middle of the waterway, but about equidistant to the extremes of navigation in terms of cruise time. Formerly owned by Guinness, the company does not appear to be wanting, and the new reception area and headquarters on the river are splendid, sporting a spread of jetties that occupy a substantial piece of the river less than a five minute walk from Carrick-on-Shannon's main street. This is a busy marina, adjacent to Carrick Craft's, and may be a bit intimidating to novice boaters. Nevertheless, the staff is helpful and provide any assistance you may need in departing or mooring. The incorporation of Emerald Star with Connoisseur Cruisers of Wroxham, England, manufacturers and operators of an elegant line of boats in Britain, France, and Belgium, adds much to the cruiser resources and services of this company.

Of the fleet of more than 230 cruisers, about half are based here, offering a very complete selection with a choice of some ten cruisers, with new ones coming into the fleet almost every year. Our first introduction to motor cruising on the Shannon–Erne was in the 29-ft. Town Star class, an ideal boat for two persons, especially beginners, to spend a week in, especially northbound through the locks of the Link. For longer periods, and if there is a third person or two children, we'd definitely move up to the new Mountain Star, a very slick 34-foot broad beam boat.

The largest of the cruisers (among the largest on the waterway) are the Shannon Star and the Glen Star, both the same dimension at 43-by-13.6-feet, and provide the ultimate in cruising for families and traveling companions. The former is luxury, with berths for only seven, whereas the latter is rated for ten (which we think would feel quite crowded after a day or so). In our view, the optimum cruiser for two couples or family of four in terms of design and price is the Lake Star class, a 32-by-12-foot craft with separate cabins and shower/toilets, well arranged lounge and two helm positions. We are less attracted to the Country Star, a forward-helm cruiser with sliding roof; it is nice for families but its limited rear view might make it difficult for boaters with little experience. The cruisers are all neat, clean, and well designed, some new, some older but well maintained. Look for new styles in the future as the association with Connoisseur Cruisers produces new lines of cruisers.

Transportation: The best air destination for Carrick-on-Shannon is Dublin, but travel to and from Belfast can be arranged and costs the same. Dublin and Belfast serve the Belturbet base equally, and the south base at Portumna is best served out of Dublin, but transport to and from Shannon airport can also be easily arranged. Transfer via coach can be set up at time of booking; the cost is IRE£16 per person each way and children under twelve years are free. Provisioning is easy at any of several stores in Carrick-on-Shannon, a short walk from the boatyard, or can be ordered ahead at the time of booking.

For river and lake details near the other Emerald Star–Connoisseur Cruisers boatyards, see the company listing in Chapters 2 and 6.

- **Crown Blue Line**
Two Bases: North & South Shannon
Carrick-on-Shannon
Co. Leitrim
Rep. of Ireland
Int'l Office: 8 Ber Street
Norwich, Norfolk, NR13EJ, England
Tel: 44-1603-630513; Fax: 44-1603-664298
E-mail: Boating@crownblueline.co.uk
Website: www.crownblueline.com
US office: 185 Bridge Plaza North, Suite 310
Fort Lee, NJ 07024
Tel: (toll free) 888-355-9491
Fax: 201-242-4476
E-mail: crownbluelineus@att.net
To contact the Carrick-on-Shannon boatyard:
Tel: 353-782-1196; Fax: 782-1196
Agents: UK: Blakes Holiday Boating; US: Great Trips Unlimited, Blakes Vacations, Le Boat, Judy Lexow Yacht Charters (see Appendix)

This large, English-based company specializes in cruising in France, with Ireland, Scotland, the Netherlands, and Germany as secondary markets. It is characterized by large luxury cruisers, medium-size luxury cruisers, and a scattering of those with more modest standards. The prices reflect this, and although class for class their Ireland-based boats rent for less than in France, they are higher than comparable cruisers on the Shannon. They are not for budget boaters, but there is no question that the cruisers are top-notch in terms of design, newness, fitting, and equipment. For two persons there are two models in Ireland, the Cirrus, and the Consort.

We recommend the former, a new cruiser whose design maximizes interior space, while the latter is sportier and has more exterior deck. For two couples or family of four or five, the sporty 33-ft. Countess with its excellent layout is hard to beat. For large luxury, it's the Classique.

As with the other lines based in Carrick-on-Shannon, the best air destination is Dublin, but travel to and from Belfast can be arranged and costs the same. Transfer via coach can be arranged at time of booking; the cost is about IRE£20 per person each way, with children under twelve free. Shannon airport transportation can also be arranged.

Crown Blue operations are located at the Rosebank Marina, downriver of the Carrick bridge. It is not easy walking distance from central Carrick, so plan to either take a taxi after grocery shopping, or order a starting supply of groceries at the time of booking. At the time of publication, Crown Blue is establishing a boatyard at Killaloe, the south end of Shannon navigation.

• Lough Ree Cruisers
North-Center Shannon at S.E. Lough Ree
Mucknagh Point, Glasson
Athlone, Co. Westmeath
Ireland
Tel/Fax: Dublin: 353-1-492-3307
Boatyard: 353-902-85256
E-mail: loughreecruisers@eirecom.net
Website: www.loughreecruisers.ie
US Agent: Le Boat (see Appendix)

Based in the Inner Loughs that lead off from the extreme southeast of Lough Ree, this small but growing fleet offers the cruisers of Connoisseur, a boat builder and fleet operator in Wroxham, England. At present there are about a dozen boats in two classes, both 37-footers set up with six berths. They are of a design more common to England's Broads than to the

The North Shannon

Shannon, with sliding roofs covering the lounge area and helm, which provide protection on rainy days but are especially pleasant for sunny days. Because Connoisseur builds some of the nicest cruisers on the waterways of Europe, be sure to inquire about any new cruisers that have been sent to the Ireland base.

Transportation is best between Dublin and the boatbase, but can be arranged to and from Shannon airport. The fare is IRE£40 for the round trip. There is rail service from and to Dublin, but from Shannon/Limerick it is time consuming, and both are a bit awkward on the Glasson end from the station to the boatyard. The scheduling of the transport is shared between Lough Ree Cruisers and Waveline Cruisers (profile follows) so make sure you make clear when you want to be picked up at Dublin or Shannon. Start days are Saturday and Wednesday.

The boatyard on Killinure Lough is a bit off the main roads, but lies only 5 miles from the pretty town of Glasson, and the three lakes, Killinure, Ballykeeran, and Coosan are scenic and tranquil. Provisioning is best handled by stopping in Glasson on the way from the airport to shop for the basic needs and enough food for two or three meals—then cruising to Ballykeeran (½ hour) or larger Athlone (1½ hours) the following day for more groceries. If traveling by means of the transfer minibus, they will stop in Glasson for clients to shop for the basic needs and food for a couple of meals.

There are nice hotels in the area, most of them quite reasonably priced, as well as B&Bs in Glasson, near the marina. Accommodations for travelers wanting to arrive a day or two before beginning to cruise can be arranged at the time of booking.

The location allows for cruise itineraries either south or north (or an elliptical one for that matter). Our inclination would be to travel south, allowing an afternoon at monastic Clonmacnois, then on into northern Lough Derg, Portumna and the nature preserve, then return north into Lough Ree, exploring as long as time permits. The best moorings for the first overnight are at the Ballykeeran Marina at the west end of the Inner Loughs (½ hour) or, proceeding a little further, westward across Lough Ree at the very pretty Hodson Bay (1 hour). Downriver, Athlone has many mooring spots, including the Jolly Mariner Marina at the north end of the city and three just above and just below the Athlone highway bridge. The next mooring south, Clonmacnois, has no facilities.

Upriver or, rather, up-lake, north of Hodson Bay there are no reliable public moorings until large Lough Ree is crossed; at the north end there is a quay and small harbor at Lanesborough, about 3½ hours from the Mucknagh Point boatyard.

• Waveline Cruisers Ltd.

North-Center Shannon at S.E. Lough Ree
Killinure Point, Glasson
Co. Westmeath, Ireland
Tel: 353-902-85711; Fax: 353-902-85716
E-Mail: waveline@iol.ie www.waveline.ie
US Agent: Great Trips Unlimited (see Appendix)

This is a relatively new cruiser company that started operation in the 1996 season, grew to eighteen cruisers within three years, plus another nine in 1998–99 and others in late 1999 and 2000. The fleet of cruisers is especially nice—modern, relatively new, all spotless, with appealing colors and layouts. The cruisers we looked at in various marinas and moorings were all especially well designed, operated by mostly Continental boaters who were very pleased with them. In sum, it is a good operation. The queen of the fleet is a 37-foot cruiser named Wavequeen well set up to sleep six people in comfort.

Transportation can be arranged at the time of booking from Dublin, Shannon, and Knock airports for IRE£40 round trip.

As noted above in the profile of Lough Ree Cruisers, above, provisioning is best handled by means of the transfer minibus stopping in Glasson for clients to shop for the basic needs and food for a couple of meals—then cruise to Athlone (1½ hours) the following day for more groceries.

There are nice hotels in the area, most of them quite reasonably priced, as well as B&Bs in Glasson, which is only 3 miles from the marina. Golfers might want to take advantage of the excellent Glasson Golf & Country Club, which can be reached from their jetty on the seventeenth hole (gear is available for rent).

Quigley's Marina on Killinure Point is just at the entry to the Inner Lakes, so the first night's mooring depends on whether you want to cruise back into the lakes before departing on the Shannon. (This is an appealing option.) If so, the mooring for the first overnight is Ballykeeran Marina at the west end of the Inner Loughs (½ hour). Alternatively, cruise westward across Lough Ree to Hodson Bay (1 hour) or, as noted in the previous paragraph, downriver to Athlone. Up Lough Ree north of the marina at Killinure Point there are no reliable public moorings until the north end of the lake is reached, where there is a quay and small harbor at Lanesborough, about 3 hours from Waveline's marina.

The area is very pretty, and just cruising around these inner lakes is a pleasure.

• Athlone Cruisers
North-Center Shannon at So. Lough Ree
Jolly Mariner Marina,
Athlone, Co. Westmeath
Ireland
Tel: 353-902-72892; Fax: 353-902-74386
E-mail: acl@wmeathtc.iol.ie
Website: www.iol.ie/wmeathtc/acl

This is a family operation that has been in business for some thirty-five years, and includes not only the cruiser fleet but also Shannon Holidays, a versatile enterprise of family and staff who know the south Shannon, Athlone, and the surroundings. Besides the boatyard that houses the fleet of about forty cruisers, the Jolly Mariner Marina comprises a restaurant, pub, a nightclub, and serves as base for the 48-seat Derg Princess that offers pleasure cruises along the Shannon and into Lough Derg.

Seven cruiser classes are available, ranging from the small and relatively simple 2+1 berth Fionnuala and Cliona to the luxury 39-ft. Bernadette that can accommodate eight. The sleeping arrangements are a bit unusual in that even the large cruiser (Bernadette) has one double cabin and six single berths, one of them convertible in the lounge. This pattern of maximum sleeping spots is in all the cruisers, except, of course the small ones where there are doubles plus a convertible. They are nevertheless well-outfitted and comfortable, ideal for families, but less so for three couples, each of whom might want double berths. Both the small craft are sport-type with canopies over the steering cockpits. The prices are very favorable, so for two or four persons we recommend going to the larger size, specifically the Sinead, a 30-foot, two-shower boat with center cockpit.

Along with the two marinas in the Inner Lakes just north of Athlone, this is the closest Shannon boatyard to Dublin (about 90 minutes by car or transport minibus). Transportation from both Dublin and Shannon airports can be arranged at the time of booking and runs IRE£30 for the round trip. Regular departures from Dublin are on Wednesday and Saturday (a taxi is £70 each way for up to three persons). Athlone is the largest town on the Shannon, and there is regular rail service between Dublin and Athlone (mostly Dublin's Heuston station, some Busaras station), plus Bus Éirean. Detailed information will be given on request at the time of booking.

Provisioning is best handled after arrival; Athlone is a good size city with numerous supermarkets, grocery stores, restaurants, and all amenities. For persons without a vehicle, a taxi ride is not expensive, or transportation to and from the grocer can be arranged on arrival. If it's late after learning the ropes and provisioning, the best first night moorings are in Athlone itself, just downriver of the boatyard. Otherwise, northbound boaters should aim for Hodson Bay, less than an hour north on the west shore of Lough Ree. If the small harbor is full, steer across lake and into the inner lakes and try private Killinure Point or the public harbor at Ballykeeran Marina. Northbound boaters leaving late afternoon should avoid travel up Lough Ree: there are no adequate mooring points before Lanesborough, some 3 hours cruising away. Before starting, be sure there is enough time before dark.

Downriver, the first good mooring (1 hour cruising) is at the ruin of monastic Clonmacnois; however, it is small and there are no amenities. One more hour beyond (2 hours from the Athlone boatyard) is Shannon Bridge, where there is an east bank quay just below the bridge and another in a narrow channel five minutes south. The village is small, but there is a grocer and pub, accessible from the bridge quai, but difficult from the channel mooring.

Cruiser companies south of Athlone are profiled in the following Chapter 6.

CHAPTER 6

The South Shannon: Athlone Southward to Killaloe

The navigation charts divide the river roughly at the southern end of the long and mostly very rural Lough Ree, with the port town of Athlone appearing on both North and South charts. It's as good a place as any to make the delineating line.

As described in the last chapter, **Athlone** is a major town on the river, located just south of the point where Lough Ree narrows to again become the Shannon. Whether it is at the north end of the South Shannon or south end of the North Shannon is immaterial—it simply lies where ERA-Maptec, the chart makers who make the navigational charts for IBRA (Irish Boat Rental Association) decided was roughly mid-way along the course and, thus, at a convenient line to fold the charts. It appears on both the South Shannon and the North Shannon charts.

The river south of Athlone winds slowly through the relatively flat countryside of the midlands, with gentle hills starting to rise on the approach to **Clonmacnois** (also spelled Clonmacnoise), the most important ancient site on the Shannon, and rightly one of Ireland's most famous. The name in Irish is *Cluain Mhic Nóis*, meaning the meadow of the sons of Nós, and it is where St. Ciarán in 548 founded what became a major center of religion, trade, crafts and politics that lasted many centuries until its final end in 1522 when it

An incredible round tower rises among the ruins of the large sixth century monastic community of Clonmacnois, south of Athlone, South Shannon

was laid to ruin by the English garrison at Athlone. The site is a wonder to visit and lies easily accessible from the Shannon moorings below. The scope of the site is remarkable, covering a village-size area on a ridge and including the remains of several churches dating from the tenth to seventeenth century, a well preserved round tower, grave slabs, high crosses and a castle, as well as a modern museum that finely displays an outstanding collection of artifacts, including one of the most beautiful high crosses in Ireland. Unlike the stone of the monastic community it surrounded, the larger village was built of wood and did not survive so long as did its gravestones. Although Clonmacnois has been the destination of travelers for over fourteen centuries, its surroundings are unsullied. It is an isolated spot, at times filled with school children, tourists and picnickers, yet nevertheless it is tranquil. From its heights along an esker ridge, the view both north and south of the River Shannon evokes a sense of times long past. Just to the south stand the ruins of a Norman castle.

A walk along the esker ridge, one of the region's many of these remains of the ice age that run across Ireland from Dublin to the west coast, brings more views of the vast midlands valley, and for flower lovers an array of esker field plants including lady's bedstraw, pyramid orchids, ribwort plantain, and quaking grass.

This is an essential stop and half a day can easily be spent. There are no supply facilities for boaters, just the mooring jetty itself and the excellent visitors center.

Half an hour downriver, **Shannonbridge**, a village of about 300, is distinguished by a handsome sixteen-arch stone bridge and the brooding riverside walls of an early nineteenth-century fortification built to defend the crossing from Napoleon who, it was feared, would invade Britain by coming in the rear door through Ireland. Napoleon never arrived, but the bastion still stands. The village is a minor stop, although the **Clonmacnoise & West Offaly Railway** offers a 5+ mile circular ride in a small coach pulled by a diesel engine through the unusual Blackwater Bog (departures every hour between 10 and 5 April 1 to October 31). The mooring is fine for overnight if you find yourself there at dark, but a better bet is to plan on Banagher or Athlone.

Southeast of Shannonbridge the **Grand Canal** joins Shannon, the canal's 36th lock facing boaters who might want to proceed toward Dublin. Because this is not a natural or connecting waterway, it is not included in the book. But depending on time, it's possible to pass through two locks and moor near the pretty town of **Shannon Harbor**, where many narrowboat renters stop to refresh.

Three miles further downriver, the neat town of **Banagher** (pronounced BAN-a-her) rises along the east bank of the river. This is a major mooring stop, the boatyard for Silver Line and the southernmost of three boatyards of Carrick Craft. Everything needed by boaters can be found: Supplies, groceries, rental fishing gear, bicycles, good restaurants and pubs, plus showers at the boat company receptions for all who need more space than the cruiser shower rooms provide. It is the place where Charlotte Bronte had her honeymoon, and where in 1842 Anthony Trollope wrote his first novel while residing in the Georgian townhouse, now the **Shannon Hotel**. The **Crank House**, another Georgian building, houses the tourist office and is easy to spot on the main street that begins less than 100 yards from the marina. Stop there to determine other places you may want to visit, especially **Clonfert Cathedral** and its outstanding doorway illustrating the essence of the art of twelfth-century stonemasons. It was generally they, not the artistic sculptors of statuary, who carved the intricate designs of stone that grace the great cathedrals, churches, abbeys, castles, and other ancient buildings of the times. It was they, often known as *White Cutters*, who translated the architecture styles into edifices, whose delicate bas relief faces, flowers, and figures are as numerous as the highly-perched gargoyles from whose mouths rainwater pours. Inquire at Crank House about transportation to **Birr Castle**, the village of **Birr, Cloghan Castle**, and fifth-century **Gallen Priory.** There is also information available at Crank House of particular interest to birders and others interested in birdlife in general. While in Banagher you might want to try **Hough's Irish Singing Pub**.

If arriving before the cruise start day, accommodations are available at the Shannon Hotel just a hundred yards from the river (Tel/Fax: +353-509-51306), or at the Crank House noted above—it functions as a quality hostel as well as housing the tourist information office, a crafts shop, art gallery and coffee shop (Tel: 509-51458). Also, the Old Forge is a B&B (Tel: 509-51504) a five-minute walk from the marina.

Below Banagher to where the Shannon is joined by the **Little Brosna River** at the **Meelick Lock**, boaters should be particularly alert to birdlife and rare flora. Together the two rivers form the **Shannon Callows**, the Brosna being the southern edge of a vast area that stretches northward and eastward to form one of the great wildlife preserves of the hemisphere, as well as an area rich in rare wild plants. Tufted sedge, purple loosetrife, and creeping bent are among the many plants of the Callows, along with the less often spotted cuckoo flower. Skylarks and sedge warblers are prolific, while corncrakes are far more difficult to see. Information on fauna and flora and the means of exploration of the Callows is available at the Crank House, Athlone. There are moorings above and below the Meelick Lock (the upriver is most attractive), but there are no other facilities.

Half an hour south of Meelick, forested **Long Island** occupies a lengthy stretch of the river and has an interesting history. It is the point where in the winter of the year 1602–03, the Chieftain of West Cork, O'Sullivan Bere, and about 1,000 followers and refugees tried to cross the Shannon. Fleeing north after having been defeated by Elizabethan forces at the battle of Kinsale, they were seeking safety and sanctuary with their ally, Hugh O'Neill, at Castle O'Rourke far to the north in Ulster. Harassed as they struggled northward from Glengarriff over the mountains, attacked as they moved slowly through the lakelands, it was on the Shannon banks that in desperation they stopped, slaughtered many of their horses to eat and make skin boats for the crossing. During their desperate fording many of the band were swept away and drowned in the flooding river. Of the near thousand who had left the area of Kinsale, by the time sanctuary was reached in Leitrim, only thirty-five souls were left: sixteen armed men, eighteen unarmed, one woman and no children.

Just downriver of Long Island is **Connaught Harbour**, noted only because it is the southern marina and boatyard for Emerald Star–Connoisseur Cruisers. From there can be seen the **Portumna Swing Bridge** that must share its opening and closing times between boaters and drivers on the highway. The times of opening are shown in Chapter 4 as well as in the Captain's Handbooks for the Southern Shannon. As previously noted, if you miss an opening, simply tie up or wait in the water for the next opening.

Ten minutes cruising south from the swing bridge, the river begins to open to form **Lough Derg**, the largest lake of the Shannon. Toward the west lies the small but, to boaters, important village of **Portumna,** with its little Castle Harbour, often crowded because of its location at the north end of Lough Derg and the many interesting places in the area to visit. *Boaters planning to overnight at Portumna harbor should arrive by mid-afternoon in the summer months.* The attractive new mooring spot surrounded by grass and trees is just a few minutes walk from **Portumna Castle**, a handsome but austere semi-fortified house that is open to the public while still being restored. Alongside the road to the castle and the town stands the **Portumna Priory**, a ruin of many rooms, some walls still standing to their original height. The extensive paths and walks through **Portumna Forest Park and Sanctuary** are easy to find and follow. Walks through the park woodlands are very worthwhile, and the wildlife and lakeshore combine to make a place of beauty and serenity—a photographers' delight. The town itself is less than a quarter mile from the harbor and although not large it has plenty in terms of supplies, as well as small restaurants and pubs. For a splurge dinner or a good pub menu, try the sprawling new **Shannon Oaks Hotel**, just down an extension of the main street. Golf is open to the public there on an eighteen-hole course.

At roughly 50 square miles, **Lough Derg** stretches beyond sight in a north-south direction, and with the numerous small towns, moorings, and points of interest can easily occupy three days or so of exploration. It is well charted and navigation markers are clear and easy to spot, but strong north or south winds can create good-sized waves. Combined with currents, when such winds blow boaters should pay close attention to their charts and travel with another cruiser nearby if possible.

Harbor and tower ruin at the village of Dromineer on the eastern shore of Lough Derg

129

*Navigation markers double
as perches for the cormorants
all along the river*

The countryside surrounding the lake is hilly and rural, much of it beautifully forested, with occasional farmsteads and sloping meadows. These, combined with the lake's expanse, create a sense of splendid isolation. Like much of the Shannon, the Erne Lakes, and in fact most of the natural waterways of this part of the world, this is a place for lying back and absorbing some of the better aspects of our planet.

As noted in the Chapter 4, Lough Derg is the fishing spot for trophy-size pike, particularly sought after by anglers from Europe who come to the Shannon for that very purpose. With the sport comes the social life, so it is not uncommon to see very large rental cruisers tied to the shores or idling along with half a dozen rods protruding while the rest of the group lounges on the upper deck. The lake is large enough that even in peak season the impact of other cruisers is minimal.

Besides the little towns that punctuate the shoreline, you may want to explore the bays and inlets, carefully studying the charts and watching the navigation markers. Eastward across the lake from Portumna (30 minutes cruising) is the little harbor and, a five-minute walk away, the village of **Terryglass**. The harbor is small with nose-in jetties, easy to get in and out of, with an associated picnic area and playground. And it is a good night mooring spot. The main street is just a handful of little shops, a grocer, and a very good pub/cafe. Also, the Old Church Gift Shop occupies a small de-consecrated chapel and is a good source for interesting arts and crafts of the area. It is important to know that there is no VAT (Value Added Tax) to pay on purchases in small private or community shops such as this, so the trouble of applying for a VAT refund on departing the country is not necessary.

Some 3 hours cruising time downlake of Terryglass on the west shore is **Williamstown Harbour**, with a narrow entry to the marina of Shannon Castle Line. There are no other facilities there. Across the lake on the southern shore of **Dromineer Harbor**, the picturesque ruin of sixteenth-century **Dromineer Castle** rises above the large marina and public moorings of the village of Dromineer. It is a neat, snug harbor surrounded by a grassy park with picnic table and playground. On a rise to the south, the **Dromineer Bay Hotel** overlooks the marina and the lake, its second floor pub and atrium particularly inviting. Ask proprietors Denis or Lily Collison (or anyone in town) about the old **John Hanly & Co. Woolen Mill**, and try to make a visit to this historic spot.

The next harbor and mooring downlake is **Garrykennedy,** about which little can be said except that it is tiny, picturesque and along with the neighboring town of **Portroe**, known for traditional Irish music in the pubs. This harbor, along with Dromineer just uplake and Mouthshannon across the lake, are ideal first and last night moorings if you are cruising in an Ireland Line or Emerald Star-Connoisseur Cruisers boat out of Killaloe.

An hour cruising time across the lake from Garrykennedy on the west shore, **Mountshannon** has the recent distinction of having won the 1998 European Blue Flag for the outstanding quality of its harbor. And it won the 1981 National Tidy Town award and seems not to have changed. It is a pretty, tidy town with a wonderful tidy marina. Its small shops and pubs offer most anything a boater needs.

Settled on the lakeshore at the foot of the low **Slieve Aughty Mountains**, this is also a village whose surroundings can be enjoyably explored. The 1845 gothic style **Roman Catholic Church** is a five-minute walk from the tree-lined main street down the Scariff Road. The **Church of Ireland**

(1785) is at the north end of the main street. Originally built in the early 1740s as a community to provide housing for workers in the linen industry, the village had to provide community buildings—a blacksmith's, livery, marketplace, and the like, so in many ways a walk around the town is like a visit to a village of the distant past. Even "modern" Mountshannon seems more like a place out of 1920s midwest America than a contemporary Irish town.

Just outside the harbor stands **Inishcealtra**, Holy Island, on which the remains of an ancient monastic community are easily spotted by its round tower and church walls. There is no mooring for hire cruisers, but the east side of the island rises abruptly and the water is deep to the shoreline so it can be approached closely for a look or photography. The only approach to visiting the island is by small boat operated from the **East Clare Heritage Centre** at the village of **Tuamgraney** (see below).

For boaters starting out from Killaloe, 2 hours to the south, or Williamstown Harbour just to the north, Mountshannon Harbour and town provide a very nice introduction to the area and to boating on Lough Derg. We especially recommend Mountshannon for the first overnight out of Killaloe. As with most of the Lough Derg harbors, although this one is fairly large it can fill up early, so don't wait until late to find a mooring.

Scariff lies south across Scariff Bay from Mountshannon, up a narrowing inlet past Cahir Island and Rinnemicrush Point and on for about three miles up the Scariff River. The charts show the river as narrow here, and it is, but it is not a problem to navigate. There is a small mooring about half way between the lake and the town harbor where it is best to moor for a short walk to the town of Tuamgraney. What is reputed to be Ireland's oldest church is still in use here, thought to have been built for King Brian Boru in AD 969. Also there is the East Clare Heritage Centre where much about the area can be learned both from displays, the staff, organized walks, and by means of a small boat to Holy Island (see above).

For a visit to Scariff town, tie up at the harbor at the end of the river navigation and take the short walk. It is a little old market town, enjoyable to wander through by virtue of its being a typical market town, simple, yet with some air of sophistication that combines farming with theater. The **Scariff Players** have won drama awards including the All Ireland Drama festival in Athlone.

Killaloe and **Ballina**, adjacent towns split by the river and crossed by a handsome bridge, are currently the south end of Shannon navigation for rental cruisers. In early 1999 a project began to extend downriver another 20 miles or so into the city of Limerick. To determine the status of the project, we suggest contacting Ireland Line or Crown Blue Line at **Killaloe**, the only cruiser bases at the extreme southern end of the waterway.

Killaloe spills down a steep hillside to the edge of the Shannon, which has again become a wide river flowing from the southern end of Lough Derg. To the east across a thirteen-arch stone bridge lies Ballina, more of a suburb of the larger town across the river because it lacks a true center. Between

Killaloe-Ballina Bridge, South Shannon, County Clare

Molly's Pub on the Shannon in Ballina, just across the river from Killaloe near the south end of navigation

the two towns, however, Ballina is the most important to cruiser renters in that it has a relatively new and very attractive public quay, a major marina, the boatyard of Ireland Line, the **Lakeside Hotel** just 100 yards from the boatyard, a small Londis supermarket that will deliver groceries to the boatyard, and the fine old **Molly's Pub**. For anyone who wants to refresh memories of America or Canada, a "ChewChew" Restaurant is near the mooring.

Together the two towns have the largest marina facilities on the Shannon–Erne Waterway system, with space for about 200 boats. Cruisers can be seen moving downriver beyond the bridge, but they are privately owned and should be operated by experienced skippers. On the Killaloe side most of the moorings are along a channel separate from the river; some are private, some public. We suggest tying up on the Ballina side where the riverside area is attractive, easy to manage and convenient. If it is full, then try across the river where it is also congenial or, if operating an Ireland Line boat, moor in their marina just 200 yards upriver on the Ballina side.

Ballina may be the best base for cruisers and crews, but it is Killaloe that should be visited, just a short walk across the bridge to the main streets. It is a town of ancient origins, having been a flourishing medieval center of trade, politics, and religion. It's a bit far to walk, but a short taxi ride takes one to an earthen fortification just north of town. Called **Beal Boru**, it is likely an ancient ring fort. Not much to see, but it makes clear the antiquity of the area. Walk the streets, visit the shops, try the pubs and cafes, and stop by **St. Flannan's Cathedral**, an unpretentious twelfth-century church. Besides its simple beauty and its intricately carved oak screen, the prize is a fragment of a stone cross bearing words in both the old Irish Ogham and Norse Runic. The Ogham reads "A Blessing upon Thogrim" and the Runic reads "Thogrim carved this cross." Also at Killaloe is the **Lough Derg Interpretive Centre** near the bridge, offering a small rendition of the area and its history.

Cruising Times

Cruising times between key points of the full length of the Shannon, as well as example itineraries, are shown in Chapter 4. The following times listed from north to south are for stretches of the South Shannon; for a total time between extremes, add the legs, e.g., between Athlone and Portumna add 2 + 3 + 3 = 8 hours. The entire Athlone–Killaloe time is 2 + 3 + 3 + 5 + 2 = 15 hours. The Lough Derg cruising time is Portumna–Killaloe: 5 + 2 = 7 hours. (See Appendix for Average Cruising Times for the entire waterway system.)

Athlone to Clonmacnois	2 hours
Clonmacnois to Banagher	3 hours
Banagher to Portumna	3 hours
Portumna to Terryglass (cross-lake)	½ hour
Portumna to Mountshannon	5 hours
Mountshannon to Killaloe	2 hours

Emerald Star–Connoisseur Cruisers and Carrick Craft, also have boatyards on the North Shannon and the Erne waterway system. Approximate one-way cruising times:

Portumna to Carrick-on-Shannon (Emerald Star–Connoisseur)	19 hours
Portumna to Belturbet (Erne) (Emerald Star–Connoisseur)	35 hours
Banagher to Knockninny (Erne) (Carrick Craft)	37 hours
Banagher to Carrick-on-Shannon (Carrick Craft)	16 hours

The Portumna Swing Bridge at the north end of Lough Derg opens at specific times to let river traffic through. It is open for roughly fifteen minutes each time, depending on river traffic. *Note:* The exact dates for which the following times are shown may vary slightly from year to year, so be sure to check at one of the boatyards.

Dates	*Monday–Saturday*	*Sunday*
Mar 14 to April 3	9:45 & 11 AM; 12:30, 2:30 & 4:30 PM	11 AM; 12:30, 2:30 & 4:30 PM
April 4 to Sept 25	9:45 & 11 AM; 12:30, 3, 5:30 & 7:30 PM	11 AM; 12:30, 3 & 4:30 PM
Sept 26 to Nov 1	9:45 & 11 AM; 12:30, 3, 5 & 6:30 PM	11 AM: 12:30, 2:30 & 4 PM
Nov 2 to Mar 13	9:45 & 11 AM; 12 PM	11 AM; 12 PM

Boat Rental Bases

As can be seen from the foregoing, the South Shannon and its great Lough Derg is an area rich with interest for cruisers, with many lake and riverside villages and moorings, monastic communities, ruins and islands. A very full week can be spent between the extremes, Athlone and Killaloe, in either direction. As with other regions of the waterway, we found no boat companies on the South Shannon that we would not be pleased to book with, nor any without an adequate selection of cruisers. As noted elsewhere, your choice is an individual one, based on where you want to cruise, whether or not the boatyard is in a town is of any importance to you, personal taste in cruiser style and appearance, and budget. However, all else being equal we nevertheless see an advantage to starting out from a boatyard that is in or near a town of interest and where there is a convenient source of supplies. From north to south these are Athlone, Banagher, Portumna, and Killaloe.

The second main factor is what your destination airport in Ireland will be. If it is Shannon airport, and if you plan a one-week itinerary up the lake and river and return, the best plan is to book with Ireland Line and cruise out of Killaloe. The cruisers are quite nice, and at a leisurely pace with stops and walks and shore explorations, a round trip up to Clonmacnois is easy, requiring 13 hours cruising each way; that's 26 hours total, an average of a little under five hours travel per day. This is ideal. Two persons will like the Birchwood 32 at a cost just slightly more than the smaller Birchwood 29; the Birchwood 35 is a good choice for four. Another choice is with Crown Blue Line at Killaloe.

If your destination airport is Dublin, then Athlone and Banagher are the closest bases, with Portumna not much farther. If you plan a week-long itinerary in the southern section and want to cruise Lough Derg and return to your starting point, the most convenient boat bases are Athlone Cruisers at Athlone and Carrick Craft and Silver Line at Banagher. The choice then depends on what cruisers appeal most and which best suit your budget.

Also out of Dublin if you want to cruise one-way, the choices are Emerald Star–Connoisseur Cruisers at Connaught Harbour on the outskirts of Portumna and, again, Carrick Craft at Banagher. Both have bases to the north at Carrick-on-Shannon and to the far north on the Erne (Belturbet and Knockninny, respectively). This is another case of simply looking through the brochures and the websites to pick the cruiser that best strikes your fancy and meets you budget.

Both companies have fine cruisers and large fleets. Of Emerald Star–Connoisseur we especially like the new Mountain Star class for four berths and Town Star, a sport-type cruiser for two persons. Carrick Craft's Kilkenny class is ideal for four, and the sporty Carlow class is great for a couple traveling light. The choice of Portumna as the southern base for a one-way trip means the longest stretch: 19 hours (four easy days) to Carrick-on-Shannon, five steady days to include Lough Key, 35 hours (six-plus days) through the Link to Belturbet, or seven days if Lough Key is included. From Banagher, subtract 3 hours from these times, but add them back for trips ending at the Knockninny base on Lower Lough Erne.

Security deposits are required by all the hire boat companies, ranging between £150 and £350 depending on the size of the vessel. This refundable deposit can be made by credit card—the charge simply not recorded unless the boat is returned damaged. An option is to purchase damage insurance.

Getting to the Boatyards

Transportation from and to Dublin and Shannon airports and Dublin ferryport can be arranged through all the hire boat companies. This is usually by means of a van, minibus, or coach that collects clients at the terminals of the principal airports. All flight arrival information must be given to the boat company, which, in turn, schedules the pickups at the appropriate arrival lounge or baggage area. Cost of one-way transportation runs about IRE£15 to IRE£20 per person, double that for round trip (called "return" by the British and Irish). This is the typical, and best, way of transport for travelers without a vehicle. Unless otherwise noted in the profiles, this means of transfer is available from the cruiser company.

As noted above, Killaloe is most convenient to Shannon airport; Williamstown Harbour isn't much farther and the cost is the same, but there is no town and no amenities there except the Shannon Castle boatyard.

Be alert to the cruising start days of the company you book with, and even to the start days of particular cruisers. Saturdays are the norm, but more and more companies are adding other days of the week, most often giving a choice between Wednesday, Friday, and Saturday.

The approach we recommend, when flexible trip scheduling is possible, is to plan to arrive in your airport destination a day or two in advance of the cruising start day. At the time you arrange transportation with the boat company, ask them about nearby hotels. A few we recommend include:

Lakeside Hotel, Killaloe
Tel: 353-61-376122; Fax: 61-376431
Paddock Hotel, Athlone, Tel: 902-72070
Prince of Wales Hotel Tel: 902-72626; Fax: 902-75658
Royal Hotel Tel: 902-72924; Fax: 902-75194

Plan for a night to orient yourselves and get over jet lag, then go to the boatyard the following day.

If planning an arrival in Dublin to cruise southward from the Athlone area, there is also rail service between Dublin (Heuston) and Athlone, as well as Bus Éirean. We suggest, however, taking the boat company transfer if you are departing for the boatyard immediately upon arrival— arranging rail or bus after all night on the jet isn't worth the few IRE£ you might save.

For visitors who choose to rent a car, no boatyards along the Shannon system are so distant from Dublin that driving to them is too inconvenient. It's only about 80 miles between Dublin and Athlone and 100 between Dublin and Portumna. Shannon airport to Killaloe is about 30 miles via Limerick.

CRUISER LINE PROFILES

The following boat rental companies are listed from north to south. Except as noted with a 44 (UK), all telephone and fax numbers below must be preceded by the Republic of Ireland country code 353.

- **Athlone Cruisers**
Central Shannon
Jolly Mariner Marina, Athlone
Tel: 353-902-72892; Fax: 353-902-74386
For the Athlone Cruisers profile and cruiser descriptions see Chapter 5.

- **Silver Line Cruisers, Ltd.**
Mid-South Shannon
The Marina, Banagher
Co. Offaly, Rep. of Ireland
Tel: 353-509-51112; Fax: 353-509-51632
E-mail: silverline@eircom.net
Website: www.silverlinecruisers.com
US Agents: Isle Inn Tours (see Appendix)

This family owned and operated company has been in business for over twenty-five years and has a fleet of some forty-five very handsome cruisers based at the convenient marina at the bottom of the main street of the town of Banagher. The boatyard, reached through a small park, is less than 200 yards from the river-end of the town center of grocery stores, restaurants, and shops. Shower and laundry facilities are available at the new reception center.

We especially like the layouts of most of the cruisers, as well as the fittings and the interiors that are appealing to the eye in the choice of finishes and fabric. And we appreciate the good quality of the kitchen and dining equipment. Every Silver Line crew we met along the waterway liked their cruisers.

All classes except the older Silver Swan and the small Silver River had dual helms, a feature that we find adds much enjoyment to cruising. In fact, the main problem with the fleet overall is that the two smaller cruisers, the two-berth Silver River sport cruiser and the four-berth Silver Swan have open steering cockpits that require folding canopies for enclosure. This is a nuisance except during long stretches of sunny days, a most unpredictable event. The classic Silver Mist, however, provides much more space for not much more money, and the Crest, Sceptre, and Crown are new and truly top-of-the-line.

Transportation can be arranged at the time of booking, and Banagher is equally accessible from Dublin and Shannon airport, although the latter is a bit shorter (2 hours from Dublin vs. 1½ hours from Shannon). The fare is about IRE£16 and £15 respectively per person one-way. There is one bus daily, but its 6 PM departure makes it impractical.

Although groceries and supplies can be ordered in advance, the stores are so near the marina that it's just as well to shop after arrival. If you plan to arrive in Banagher a day early, tell the company at the time of booking and ask that a room reservation be made. The town offers a very pleasant stay.

Downriver, a good first night mooring point is Portumna Harbour (3 hours). See Portumna in the highlights in the preceding section, and also check the openings of the Portumna Swing Bridge. For an early stop or if concerned about late arrival at the busy little Portumna Harbour, the mooring above the top of the weir at Meelick is very nice, although there are no other facilities (1 hour). Traveling upriver, try Shannon Bridge (3 hours) because the next mooring, Clonmacnois (+1 hour), is not ideal for overnight mooring, and the next is Athlone (+1 hour).

- **Carrick Craft**
Mid-South Shannon (also North Shannon & Erne)

The Marina, Banagher
Co. Offaly, Rep. of Ireland
International booking (No. Ireland):
Tel: +44-28-3834-4993; Fax: +44-283-834-4995
E-mail: sales@carrickcraft.com
Website: www.cruise-ireland.com
Agents: UK: Blakes; US: Blakes Vacations, Great Trips
Unlimited (see Appendix)
See the main company profile and cruiser descriptions in Chapter 5.

A fleet of over 150 rental cruisers makes this not only one of the largest cruiser operations on the Shannon–Erne, but also provides an extensive and good choice of rental craft. There are at present eight classes of cruisers to choose from, ranging from the very small, economy Dublin class to the large (eight berth), elegant Clare class. Unless you are on a very tight budget and plan to travel light, we can't recommend the little 24-ft. Dublin. Instead, for two persons we suggest a small step up to the 27-ft. Carlow class, which has a better overall design as well as more interior space. For three to four persons on a slim budget, the Kerry class is fine except that it has a single aft steering position open to the elements unless the fabric hood is erected.

We took a 34-ft. Kilkenny class from Banagher up to Carrick and found it to be a delight: easy to steer, with dual helm and modern design. It is perfect for two couples or a family of four or five needing two private cabins, each with shower and toilet. For something special, consider the newest addition to the fleet, the deluxe 6+2 berth Waterford, a handsome, well equipped cruiser of the latest design.

The Kilkenny (4+2 berth) and the Carlow (2+) are usually the cruisers reserved for one-way north trips through the Link for drop-off at the Erne base at Knockninny. There is a supplemental drop-off fee of IRE£45 for one way travel.

The Banagher marina is at the bottom of the main street

of the town, less than 200 yards from the commercial center of grocery stores, restaurants, and shops. Shower and laundry facilities are at the reception center.

Banagher is equally convenient from Shannon and Dublin and transport can be arranged at time of booking; the cost is about IRE£16 per person each way and is the same Dublin and Shannon.

Week-long round-trip cruises can be easily worked out for either direction, or a one-way cruise to drop off the boat at Carrick Craft's northern base at Carrick-on-Shannon and, for a two week journey, on up to the Erne base at Knockninny on Upper Lough Erne north of the Link.

Assuming a mid-afternoon departure, a good first night mooring point downriver is Portumna Harbour (3 hours). Refer to the highlights in the preceding section, and also check the openings of the Portumna Swing Bridge. In a pinch for time, the mooring above the top of the weir at Meelick is very nice, although there are no other facilities (1 hour). Traveling upriver, try Shannon Bridge (3 hours), but avoid Clonmacnois 1 hour beyond for an overnight mooring; if there is enough daylight, plan on Athlone (+1 hour) instead.

• Emerald Star–Connoisseur Cruisers

Bases: So. Shannon, No. Shannon River Erne
South Base: Connaught Harbour/Portumna
Portumna Tel: 353-509-41120
Booking/information Tel: 353-78-20234; Fax: 78-21433
E-mail: info@emerald-star.com
Website: www.emeraldstar.ie
OR www.connoisseurcruisers.co.uk
Agents: UK: Blakes Holiday Boating; US: Great Trips Unlimited, Blakes Vacations, Jody Lexow Yacht Charters, Le Boat (see Appendix)
See the main company profile in Chapter 5.
The incorporation of Emerald Star with Connoisseur Cruisers

of Wroxham, England, the manufacturers and operators of an elegant line of boats in Britain, France, and Belgium, adds much to the cruiser resources and services of this company.

Of the fleet of more than 230 cruisers, about one-third are based here. This offers a very complete selection with a choice of some ten cruiser styles, with new ones coming into the fleet almost every year. Our first introduction to motor cruising on the Shannon–Erne was in little 29-ft. Town Star class, an ideal boat for two persons, especially beginners, especially northbound through the locks of the Link. For longer periods, and if there is a third person or two children, we'd definitely move up to the new Mountain Star, a very fine 34-foot broad beam boat.

The largest of the cruisers are the Shannon Star and the Glen Star, both the same dimension at 43-by-13½-feet. They are among the largest on the waterway, and provide the ultimate in cruising for families and traveling companions. The former is luxury, with berths for only seven, whereas the latter is rated for ten (which we think would feel quite crowded after a day or so). Look for new styles in the future as the association with Connoisseur Cruisers produces new lines of cruisers.

The southernmost base of this large company is just north of the swing-bridge at the town of Portumna at the north end of Lough Derg. The location is ideal in that it allows for travel in either direction: South for an exploration of Lough Derg with its remarkable birdlife, as well as good fishing and access to the pretty and interesting towns of the Derg lakeshore. Week-long round-trip cruises can be easily worked out for either direction, or a one-way cruise to drop off the boat at Emerald Star-Connoisseur's northern base at Carrick-on-Shannon and, for a two-week journey, on up to the Erne base at Belturbet north of the Link. There is an IRE£50 drop fee for one-way.

Transportation: Portumna is closer to Shannon than it is to Dublin, but both are convenient. Transportation can be arranged at time of booking; the cost is IRE£16 per person each way and is the same Dublin and Shannon. Children under twelve years free. Travelers who want a car awaiting them at the end of the cruise can arrange through the company for delivery, but it's usually best to make rental car arrangements in the US or Canada before departure.

A starting supply of groceries can be ordered at the time of booking, and are also available in Portumna. The taxi fare is about IRE£4 between town and boatyard, or, more conveniently, cruise from the boatyard downriver fifteen minutes to the public mooring. It's then a short walk to the Portumna town center, well worth a visit.

Downriver, an ideal first night mooring after a mid-afternoon departure is at Portumna or across the lake at Terryglass. Both are fairly small marinas so in high season try to arrive early. Check the opening times of the Portumna Swing Bridge just south of the marina. Upriver, Meelick Lock is a good stop. Arrive early enough that the lockkeeper is on duty, pass through the lock, and moor toward the upper end of the weir.

• Shannon Castle Line
South Shannon at S.W. Lough Derg
Williamstown Harbor
Whitegate, Co. Clare
Rep. of Ireland
Tel: 353-61-927042, 353-61-927475; Fax: 353-61-927426
E-mail: sales@shannoncruisers.com
Website: www.shannoncruisers.com
Agents: UK: Blakes; US: Blakes Vacations, Great Trips Unlimited (see Appendix).

Regrettably, we passed by the narrow entry to the Williamstown boatyard on an afternoon plagued with squalls locally thought, or joked about, to be the unusual remnants of an "American" hurricane. We pointed out that it was spawned off Africa and developed in the Caribbean. In any case, although we did not visit the Shannon Castle marina, we looked at many of their cruisers and talked with boaters at other moorings. The Shannon 29 is ideal for a couple, the 31 Sports is ideal for four, and the six-berth Shannon Super Eight Sports is one of the nicest cruisers of the waterway. Their new Shannon 38 Leisure will likely be an excellent luxury choice.

What we took in of the marina (and interviewed others about) is that it is quite isolated, so provisions need to be arranged for in advance. Transportation is set up at the time of booking, and the location is most easily accessible from Shannon airport, although transport from Dublin is possible. If planning arrival a day or more before your cruise date, stay in Killaloe or nearby Mt. Shannon. Hotel arrangements can be made at the time of booking.

Down-lake, good moorings for the first night out are at Mountshannon (1 hour) and, across Lough Derg, at Dromineer (½ hour) where a nice restaurant and pub overlook the bay. Uplake, the first good overnighter is 4 hours away at Portumna, a small harbor that fills up early. Agents: UK: Blakes; US: Great Trips Unlimited, Blakes Vacations (see Appendix).

• Ireland Line Cruisers
South Shannon at So. Lough Derg
Killaloe/Ballina
Co. Clare, Rep. of Ireland
Tel: 353-61-375011; Fax: 353-61-375331
E-mail: info@irelandlinecruisers.com
Website: www.irelandlinecruisers.com
US Agent: Great Trips Unlimited (see Appendix)

After twenty years of operation the former Derg Line Cruisers was bought a few years ago by its principal employees Raymond Molloy and Billie and Maria Carroll. Their hearts and efforts are committed to keeping the venerable company as a key player in the cruiser business, and seem to be succeeding well. The location very near Shannon airport near the extreme south end of Shannon navigation is ideal for cruising the entire Lough Derg, with week-long itineraries as far north as the monastic community of Clonmacnois and on to Athlone. Couple this with the boatyard being a six-minute walk from the main street of the lovely town of Killaloe, 300 yards from a small supermarket, 200 yards from Molly's Pub, and 100 yards from the appealing Lakeside Hotel and the ingredients are all there.

Renamed Ireland Line Cruisers, there is a fleet of about twenty-six cruisers of which half are quite new, nine are of moderate age and four that will likely soon be retiring and replaced. The cruisers are all well supplied and equipped, including binoculars, a compass and, most useful, depthfinders (which are not supplied by all companies). There is a wide range of sizes and layouts, starting with the little Birchwood 29 up to the luxury 12-meter, eight-berth Derg 40, especially splendid for six persons. Although the Birchwood 29 is a nice cruiser for two, we suggest stepping up to the Birchwood 320 at a cost just slightly more. The six-berth Birchwood 35 would be our choice for four. Depth finder and cell phones on the cruisers are a definite plus.

The location of the boatyard makes preparation and arrangements easy. Groceries can be ordered in advance or, better, walk to the small Londis supermarket, shop, and they will deliver to the boat. They also have a deli, fishing gear, hardware, and phone & fax service. Accommodations, in case you want to take up the good suggestion of arriving a day or so before cruising, include the Lakeside (Tel: 353-61-376122; Fax: 61-376431) and, across the river on the northern outskirts of Killaloe, Kincora Hall (Tel: 353-61-376000; Fax: 376665).

This is an ideal situation for anyone coming into Shannon airport (or driving). Transportation can be arranged at the time of booking, at a cost from Shannon of about IRE£15 and from Dublin (a long way) of £65 one-way per person. There is rail service consisting of well over a dozen departures daily between Dublin (Heuston Station) and Limerick—check before departure to make sure that the train stops at Birdhill (2 miles from Killaloe). There is also regular bus service between the two cities, also stopping at Birdhill.

The river northward is gentle and broadens to become southern Lough Derg. The best first night mooring after a mid-afternoon departure is up the river and across Scariff Bay to Mountshannon, about 2 hours. Alternatives are across the lake to the east shore harbors at Garrykennedy ($\frac{1}{2}$ hour from Mountshannon, 2 hours from Killaloe) and Dromineer (1 hour from Mountshannon, $2\frac{1}{2}$ hours from Killaloe). All are very good, but if you need more provisions, Mountshannon is the larger town.

Cruiser companies north of and including Athlone are profiled in the preceding chapter.

Ireland Line and Silver Line cruisers moored at Mountshannon Village harbor off Lough Derg

Appendices

1. How to Contact the Agents

The hire boat companies profiled throughout this book are usually open to direct contact from prospective clients and will respond with brochures, prices, and other information. Some provide both contact and booking information on websites. But to consolidate information (and booking) from a single source, consult the following list of agents.

If contacting more than one US agent representing the same boat rental company it's wise to compare prices. If charged, a modest flat booking fee or commission of 5% or so may be a reasonable addition for US agents to charge above direct prices in order to help cover their personal service.

US AGENTS

Great Trips Unlimited
Tel: 888-239-9720, 503-297-3516; Fax: 503-297-5308
E-mail: admin@gtunlimited.com
Website: www.gtunlimited.com
Agent for Blakes, which includes Emerald Star–Connoisseur Cruisers, Carrick Craft, Lochside Cruisers, Shannon–Erne Line, Shannon Castle Line, and Shannon Sailing. Also, Ireland Line Cruisers & Waveline Cruisers.

Blakes Vacations
Tel: 800-628-8118; Fax: 847-244-8118
E-mail: blakes1076@aol.com

Website: www.blakesvacations.com
Agent for Emerald Star–Connoisseur Cruisers, Carrick Craft, Lochside Cruisers, Shannon Castle Line, and Shannon Sailing.

Le Boat
Tel: 800-922-0291
E-mail: leboatinc@worldnet.att.net
Website: www.leboat.com
Agent for Emerald Star–Connoisseur Cruisers, Locaboat Ireland Ltd., Lough Ree Cruisers, and Crown Blue Line.

Jody Lexow Yacht Charters
Tel: 800-662-2628; Fax: 401-845-8909
E-mail: jlyv@edgenet.net
Agent for Emerald Star-Connoisseur and Lough Ree Cruisers.

Isle Inn Tours
Tel: 800-237-9376, 703-683-4800; Fax: 703-683-4812
E-mail: isleinn@msn.com
Website: www.isleinntours.com
Agent for Silver Line Cruisers.

UK Agents

Blakes Holiday Boating
Tel: 011-44-1603-739400
E-mail: boats@blakes.co.uk
Website: www.blakes.co.uk
Agent for most cruiser lines

2. Government Tourist & Waterways Offices

Telephone Country Code: International access code +353
Example: To contact the Irish Tourist Board (Dublin) from the US and Canada, dial 011-353-1602-4000

Irish Tourist Board
345 Park Avenue, 17th floor
New York, NY 10154
Tel: 800-223-6470; 212-418-0800;
Fax: 212-371-9052
Website: www.ireland.travel.ie

Bord F·ilte
Baggott Street Bridge
Dublin 2
Rep. of Ireland
Tel: 353-1602-4000; Fax: 1602-4100

Shannon–Erne Waterways Promotion
Ballinamore,
Co. Leitrim, Rep. of Ireland
Tel: 353-784-4855; Fax: 784-4856
E-mail: shannonernepromo@tinet.ie
Website: www.Shannon–Erne.com
OR www.waterwayholidays.com

Telephone Country Code: International access code +44
Example: To contact the Northern Ireland Tourist Board (Belfast) from the US and Canada, dial 011-44-123-223-0036. Any "0" as a first number in a prefix is used only on domestic calls.

Northern Ireland Tourist Board
551 Fifth Avenue, 7th Floor
New York, NY 10176-0799
Tel: 800-326-0036; Fax: 212-922-0099
Websites: www.homepages.iol.ie/~discover/ni
OR www.visitbritain.com/activities/waterways/ireland

Northern Ireland Tourist Board
St. Anne's Court, 59 North Street
Belfast BT1 1NB
Tel: 44-123-223-1221; Fax: 123-224-0960
E-mail: info@nitb.com www.ni-tourism.com
(Links to cruising & cruisers)
(Note: Northern Ireland's telephone code is +44, the same as
the rest of the UK.)

British Tourist Authority (BTA)
551 Fifth Avenue, Suite 701
New York, NY 10176-0799
Tel: 800-462-2748, 212-986-2200
5915 Airport Road, Suite 120
Mississauga, Ont. L4V 1T1
Tel: 888-847-4885, 905-405-1840;
Fax: 905-405-1835
Websites: www.usagateway.visitbritain.com
OR www.visitbritain.com

Fermanagh District Council
Co. Fermanagh/Southwest general
Tel: 011-44-28-6632-3110
Websites: www.fermanagh.gov.uk/tourist.htm OR
www.fermanagh-online.com/tourism/activities/cruising.htm

3. Other Contacts

- **Narrowboat Companies** (Not profiled in this guide)
  Riversdale Barge Holidays, Ballinamore (Shannon–Erne
  Link) Tel: 353-78-44122
  Celtic Canal Cruisers, Tullamore, Offaly (S.E. Rep. of
  Ireland) Tel: 353-506-21861

Car Rentals

Most of the mainline companies such as Hertz, Avis, and
Budget have operations in Ireland. An Irish company with
an information and booking office in the US is also very
good, has a wide selection, numerous offices in both the
Republic and Northern Ireland, and is competitive in price:
  Dan Dooley Rent-a-Car
  US & Canada Tel: 800-331-9301
  Ireland Tel: 353-62-53392

Also in addition to mainline car rental companies there
are a number of excellent "brokers" or agents that own no
fleet of vehicles, but contract with both US and European
fleet owners, often well discounted. These include contracts
with the major companies.

Auto Europe (Maine) Tel: 800-223-5555, 207-842-2000
Europe by Car (Republic only; New York)
  Tel: 800-223-1516
ITS (Florida) Tel: 800-521-0643
Kemwell Holiday Autos (New York) Tel: 800-678-0678
Rob Liddiard Travel (California) Tel: 800-272-3299

Vacation Rentals

In the US
Great Trips Unlimited (Republic & Northern)
Tel: (toll free) 888-239-9720

E-mail: admin@gtunlimited.com
Website: www.gtunlimited.com (Also a cruiser agent.)

Lismore Tours, Inc. (Republic)
Tel: 800-547-6673, 212-685-0100; Fax: 212-685-0614
E-mail: lismore.com
Website: www.lismore.com

In the Republic of Ireland

Irish Tourist Board
Website: www.ireland.travel.ie
Central Reservations Tel: 800-398-4376 (This rings toll-free at the reservations office in Killorglin, County Kerry. Hours are 8:00 AM to 8:00 PM, 5 hours ahead of EST)
E-mail: gulliver@fexco.ie

Elegant Ireland (Throughout Ireland)
Tel: 011-353-1-475-1665; Fax: 1-475-1012
E-mail: info@elegant.ie
Website: www.elegant.ie

Killaloe Holiday Village (Lakeside County Clare)
Tel: 011-353-1-668-3534; Fax: 1-660-6465

Lough Ree Enterprises (Lakeside, central Shannon)
Tel & Fax: 353-1-492-3307

Portavolla Leisure Lodges (Banagher, South Shannon)
Tel: 353-23-33110, 353-509-51206
Website: www.ichh.ie/offaly.htm

Trident Holiday Homes (Throughout Ireland)
Tel: 353-1-668-3534; Fax: 1-660-6465
E-mail: reservations@thh.ie

Appendices

In Northern Ireland

Rural Cottage Holidays Ltd.
(Northern Ireland Tourist Board)
Tel: 011-44-28-9024-1100
E-mail: rural.cottages@nitb.com
Website: www.travel-ireland.com/cottages/index.htm
In North America contact the N.I.T.B. for a catalog:
800-326-0036

Crom Cottages, National Trust (Upper Lough Erne)
Tel: 011-44-28-6773-8118
Central Reservations in England Tel: 011-44-1225-791199

Belle Isle Estate (Upper Lough Erne)
Tel: 011-44-28-6638-7231
In US Tel: (toll free) 888-239-9720
E-mail: accommodation@belleisle-estate.com
Website: www.belleisle-estate.com

Fermanagh District Council (Southwest general)
Tel: 011-44-28-6632-3110
Website: www.fermanagh.gov.uk/tourist.htm

Manor House Marine & Cottages (Lower Lough Erne)
Tel: 011-44-28-6662-8100
E-mail: cruising@manormarine.com
Website: www.manormarine.com

Tully Bay Marina & Cottages (Lower Lough Erne)
Tel: 011-44-28-6864-1737; Fax: 28-6864-1737
E-mail: helen@boatingireland.com
Website: www.boatingireland.com

4. Cruiser Company Locations

THE ERNE WATERWAY

Belleek	Belleek Charter Cruising
Lisnarick	Aghinver Boat Company
Blaney	Erincurrach Cruising
Killadeas	Manor House Marine
Enniskillen	Lochside Cruisers
Knockninny Quay	Carrick Craft
Bellanaleck Quay	Erne Marine
Lisbellaw	Carrybridge Boat Company
Belturbet	Emerald Star–Connoisseur Cruisers

THE LINK

Ballinamore	Locaboat Ireland

NORTH SHANNON

Lough Key	Tara Cruisers
Knockvicar/Coothall	Shannon Erne Waterway Holidays Ltd.
Carrick-on-Shannon	Carrick Craft
	Emerald Star–Connoisseur Cruisers
	Crown Blue Line
Glasson, Lough Ree	Lough Ree Cruisers
	Waveline Cruisers
Athlone	Athlone Cruisers

SOUTH SHANNON

Banagher	Carrick Craft
	Silver Line Cruisers
Portumna	Emerald Star–Connoisseur Cruisers
Williamstown	Shannon Castle Line
Killaloe	Ireland Line Cruisers

5. Average Cruising Times (in Hours)

	BELLEEK	ENNISKILLEN	BELTURBET	BALLYCONNELL	BALLINAMORE	LEITRIM	CARRICK-ON-SHANNON	DROMOD	ROOSKY	TARMONBARRY	LANESBOROUGH	ATHLONE	SHANNONBRIDGE	BANAGHER	PORTUMNA	SCARRIFF
ENNISKILLEN	5															
BELTURBET	9	4														
BALLYCONNELL	12	7	3													
BALLINAMORE	15	10	6	3												
LEITRIM	22	16	13	10	7											
CARRICK-ON-SHANNON	23	18	14	11	8	1										
DROMOD	25	20	16	13	10	3	2									
ROOSKY	26	21	17	14	11	4	3	1								
TARMONBARRY	28	23	19	16	13	6	5	3	2							
LANESBOROUGH	29	24	20	15	12	7	6	4	3	1						
ATHLONE	32	27	23	20	17	10	9	7	6	4	3					
SHANNONBRIDGE	34	29	25	22	19	12	11	9	8	6	5	2				
BANAGHER	36	31	27	24	21	14	13	11	10	8	7	4	2			
PORTUMNA	39	34	30	27	24	17	16	14	13	11	10	7	5	3		
SCARRIFF	43	38	34	31	28	21	20	18	17	15	14	11	9	7	4	
KILLALOE	43	38	34	31	28	21	20	18	17	15	14	11	9	7	4	2